YOUR LIFE - YOUR WAY

Practical Tips and Reflections

JOY NUGENT

Inquiries and Book Orders should be addressed to:

www.soultalksbooks.com

Email: joy.nugent@internode.on.net
Phone: (213) 814-3974
Address: 500 Terry Francois Street San Francisco, CA 94158

Rev. date: 03/23/2022

YOUR LIFE - YOUR WAY

Practical Tips and Reflections

Contents

Section 4

Foreword

Joy Nugent has worked as a palliative care nurse for thirty years. She brings a wealth of knowledge and experience to her most recent book, Your Life – Your Way. Joy writes from a place of practical insight and a wisdom that has come from deep reflection on the dying journey.

This book is filled with essential information for anyone who is navigating the time before death. It will be a wonderful resource for patients who are in palliative care, their loved ones and their carers.

Being present when a person is dying opens us to a whole range of feelings and while there is often fear, ignorance about what to do or how to assist, feelings of helplessness about the terminal condition, there is also a sense of awe and reverence for the whole process, the mystery of it. It is a sense of being with the greatest event in this person's life, their leaving this world for the next. One can think of it like being born.

Yet death anxiety is very real. Joy helps the reader here by her discussion of practical matters such as the Advance Care Directive, how to plan for the last years of life, how to do a life review, and what needs to be considered in plans for personal care.

In the midst of the inevitability of death, which none of us escapes, there is also a sense that it is part of a natural process and everything is going to be ok. Through the lens of her extensive experience, Joy reveals what needs to be thought about in regard to care for the whole person. Holistic care includes spiritual, intellectual, emotional and physical care.

Using stories she shares what is helpful to know and to do for the person around the time of death. She also shares what is needed for post death management both practically and spiritually, for family and carers. Care during the time of bereavement and grief is also discussed with the understanding that comes with many years of lived experiences.

When one accompanies a dying person on this journey Joy emphasises that the most important gift we bring is ourself and our unconditional love while not underestimating the importance of knowledge and experience.

There are many pearls of wisdom in this book and it fills a space in the literature where such practical, human and spiritual insights are surely needed today

Elizabeth Keane PhD

Author: Amazing Encounters: Direct Communication from the Afterlife

Foreword

A remarkable compendium reflecting the authority of half a lifetime's active, professional presence at the bedside of dying persons, bringing comfort, support and new confidence to patients, families, and carers.

 This book speaks to the unique character of each final human journey enfolding a wide philosophy of care and a comprehensive range of practical measures with which to address the physical, emotional, and spiritual needs of those facing terminal illness.

This book contains a wealth of wisdom and guidance for those experiencing the last phase of life and for those professionals privileged to be members of their caring team.

Conquering the fear of death and being an active participant in all of life has wide ranging benefits for humanity.

Emeritus Professor Ian Maddocks AM former professor of palliative care at Flinders University, Adelaide, South Australia. Senior Australian of the Year 2013 and a passionate advocate for world peace.

SECTION 1

Introduction

From a background of private palliative care nursing, I feel compelled to empower people who are entering the last phase of life by disease, old age, or accident to take responsibility for their life as much as possible. To this end what follows are tips from the very simple and practical to the profound. I cared for people in their own homes and encouraged them to work out their own care plans – acknowledging that it was their life, their values and life journey. When people are paying for a service, they need their needs met as they see them. I learned much and recommend a different approach to care for the last phase of life which encourages self-responsibility.

In 2018 I founded the charity Soul Talks Incorporated in my home state of South Australia. The objective is to promote the prevention and treatment of death anxiety and the relevant symptoms of this mental distress by facilitating end of life preparations – e.g., Advance Care Directive preparation. I have also founded a for-profit company Hunab Ku Pty Ltd to support this charity and have put in place a legacy for this work to continue.

My story is written in three books I published: *As Good as Goodbyes Get – A Window into Death and Dying, My Way – One nurse's passion for end of life* and *Parting the Veil – Reflections on Soul.* I see death as a graduation from the lessons and experiences of a lifetime. I believe in the continuation of the soul energy which leaves the body when a person dies. I also believe in reincarnation and that we have the ability to learn from past lives and remain connected to the unseen world. Pierre Teilhard de Chardin – visionary theologian and scientist wrote:

> We are not human beings
>
> having a spiritual experience
>
> We are spiritual beings having
>
> a human experience

My mentor and spiritual guide is Florence Nightingale who was the most educated woman of her time. This quote inspires me:

> As each individual embodies unique qualities that cannot be duplicated, it would not be consistent with God's benevolent nature to obliterate that being.
>
> Because it is God's plan to raise mankind from imperfection to perfection, death must initiate a different mode of existence, one that allows for continued development.

It is my earnest wish for all people to realise the benefits to be gained when self-responsibility and self- healing are encouraged in Aged Care Facilities. Florence Nightingale recommended that all sick should be cared for at home. By following what I have shared in this publication this may indeed become a reality.

I honour and give thanks to my teachers who are too many to name and indeed span this world and the next!

When wishes are known and documented, as they are in this publication, a transfer to a provider of advanced care is made more smoothly if needed. I do not prescribe to any religion and agree with these words from Jean Houston the American author involved in the "human potential movement."

Christianity declares that God is not separate from this world but continuously creates it anew so that we move and have our being in God.

Islam affirms that the entire universe is continually coming into being and that each moment is a new "occasion" for Allah to create the whole universe.

Hinduism proclaims that the entire universe is a single body that is being continually danced into creation by a divine Life-force or Brahman.

Buddhism asserts that the entire universe arises freshly at every moment in an unceasing flow of co-dependent origination where everything depends upon everything else.

Taoism states that the Tao is the "Mother of the Universe" and is the inexhaustible source from which all things rise and fall without ceasing.

Confucianism views our universe as a unified and interpenetrating whole that is sustained and nourished by the vitality of the Life-force or chi.

Indigenous peoples declare that an animating wind or Life-force blows through all things in the world and there is aliveness and sacred power everywhere.

A major stream in Western thought portrays the universe as a single, living creature that is being continually regenerated and is evolving toward higher levels of complexity and consciousness.

Simply put I believe in the religion of love.

Advance Care Directive Considerations

In many countries, legislation has been passed to give legal effect to a person's future wishes and instructions for health care. An Advance Care Directive invites you to state what medical interventions you wish to avoid and what specific instructions you have on the place of care and what aesthetic needs such as being in nature, having fresh flowers in your room and a view of the sky you enjoy. All people have their own way of being in the world. Some we refer to as "old soul" and others as perhaps "new souls."

The purpose of an Advance Care Directive is to communicate with the health team so that the person's wishes are clear and can be honoured as much as possible. Quality of life can be improved by health care teams partnering early with a person (and then with the substitute decision maker). End-of-life care planning can avoid traumatic or unwanted treatment or procedures when the person is dying; assists or relieves the person or family of difficult life or death decisions during a crisis or emergency; and supports a person to die as they have communicated.

You are responsible for your life, achievements, and personal growth. It is important to begin this planning process while you are still mentally able to, and to consider what is important and a priority.

> What is important to me?
>
> What outcomes of care do I wish to avoid?
>
> What health care do I prefer?
>
> Where do I wish to live?
>
> What other things do I want, or what personal arrangements do I prefer?
>
> What dying wishes do I have?
>
> What health care and treatments do I refuse?
>
> Who do I trust and want to make decisions for me if I am unable to, people who will follow and respect my wishes?

This book takes a holistic health approach to identifying these needs and wishes, giving pointers to help you identify your key decisions and take self-responsibility as opposed to letting someone else make the decisions. It has been described as a Living Will. An important question to ask yourself is: "How do I wish to be remembered?" Giving and receiving of love are the highest achievement. Finding words to describe your wishes so they communicate with the family, the substitute decision maker and the health team can be a difficult, challenging but joyous process.

The heath team, (this includes ambulance/paramedics, doctors, nurses, and all health staff), are legally bound to understand these wishes and refusals. It is important to consider if quality of life is your preference or whether you prefer quantity of life at all costs. It is important to consider if medical procedures will afford you more benefits than burdens. The heath team is protected by law if acting in good faith in following the Advance Care Directive. If there is ambiguity, or differing opinions on how to proceed, there must be consultation with you if you are able or with your substitute decision maker. In most cases/ countries, there are also mechanisms for resolving any disagreements.

As it is a legal document, it has to be completed properly and formally signed and witnessed. There is only one original document, but copies can be formally certified and given to the family, substitute decision makers, and to the doctor and health team.

What is most important is to appreciate that death is a soul journey and may be viewed as a terminus where one way of life is left behind for another which is larger. Whatever the path that is taken to grow spiritually wisdom traditions past and present will have an influence. To repeat the words of Sufi mystic Rumi: "There are many lamps but only one light."

A good death has been described as dying with a love of life rather than a 'poor me' with feelings of despair, dejection, and sensing no soul connection.

Some disabilities to consider:

- Not able to contribute to family/society

- Unable to feed myself naturally, dress, walk or talk

- Burdensome treatments without real benefits

- Not able to communicate

- Chronic incurable pain

- Unable to breathe without mechanical assistance

- Loss of control over bowel and bladder

- Not able to recognise my family

- Paralysis of parts of the body

- Permanent coma

This is an example of a broad statement you may wish to consider:

If I have an irreversible illness and can no longer care for myself, I only want those treatments that make me comfortable, relieve pain and preserve my dignity according to prevailing standards of palliative care even though any of these treatments may have the effect of shortening my life. I do not want any operative procedures, or the insertion of any form of tube into my body for the purpose of hydration or nutrition.

A Deeper Dive for Those Seeking to Understand the Meaning and Purpose of Life

In this book I have endeavoured to be mindful of the traditional values and beliefs of Eastern and Western societies. In this context, bowing to feelings of loss and acknowledging the grieving process may seem inappropriate when God's will is a fundamental belief governing a person's religious faith. Personal feelings may seem an indulgence in the light of God's plan for a person. Some Asian cultures may place a higher importance in restraining from showing emotions in the interest of maintaining harmonious relationships which support the greater good.

However, understanding that bereavement and mourning assist in the understanding of other life events allows a person, regardless of culture, to be more fully present with those who are experiencing a loss and dealing with that loss in whatever way is appropriate for them. During our life we are often confronted with feelings of loss and grief. Some of these losses can be small losses, such as when we leave our parents and go to school. Other losses can include divorce or the death of a loved one.

To understand the grief process and how it can assist a person to develop self-understanding, it is important to have some awareness that we are more than just a physical being. The hospice philosophy adopts a holistic approach to care, that is, it considers the physical, intellectual, emotional, and spiritual aspects of a person. By understanding and caring for someone's feelings a person begins the journey to wholeness. Sogyal Rinpoche, the great Tibetan Buddhist teacher, says that people heal their spirit in death and that an honest, unshrinking laying bare of emotion is central to transformation. This is what he refers to as coming to terms with life or dying a good death.

The British approach to feelings during the Victorian era was very much a 'stiff upper lip'. All topics of a sensitive nature were avoided. Topics that may arouse strong feelings, such as death and dying, were not discussed in society. Women and children were often excluded from the rituals surrounding death and burial. The intention behind this was that men were protecting them from things that might upset them. However, this exclusion often left women's and children's feelings unexpressed and buried. Subsequent losses were treated in the same way, so that as the years went by the sublimated grief from the losses was accumulated and, in some instances, consumed lives and stunted emotional and spiritual growth.

In other cultures, it is thought that it might invite bad luck to share a person's misfortune or loss on a personal level, and so death is not talked about. Many Indigenous cultures have developed a formal structure of ritual and ceremony that permits the expression of feelings and so enables healing to take place. In some Middle Eastern countries, religious beliefs encourage quite dramatic displays of grief, and people weep and wail for days after someone dies.

Palliative care encourages ritual and ceremony, because actions go beyond words and speak directly to the mind or soul. The goal of grief work, which is an integral part of palliative care, is to acknowledge the importance of mourning and bereavement so a person can eventually let go and re-invest energy into new activities or relationships.

As society becomes more individualised and international, 'world-wide individuals' are identifying with others without having had direct contact with them. The death of Princess Diana is an example where people from all over the world spontaneously gathered and shared their loss through ritual and peer support. However, throughout Western society, there also seems to be an unwritten law that a person must 'move on' as quickly as possible after the death of a loved one. In reality there is always a bond and contact with those who have died is the subject of books such as "Amazing Encounters with the Afterlife" by Elizabeth Keane PhD and books written on mediumship.

Much of what has been considered so far concerns a common approach to end-of-life issues. However, for some a deeper dive into becoming aware of who they are from a soul perspective is welcomed. For example, a person sees the world not as it is but rather as they are. Thoughts and feelings tend to be projected onto another person or object as a way of recognising what is below their own conscious mind which readily recognises what can be seen and felt with the senses. It is my belief that the purpose of life is to learn, to grow, to heal, to contribute and to quote mythologist Joseph Campbell: "If you do follow your bliss you put yourself on a kind of track that has been there all the while, waiting for you, and the life that you ought to be living is the one you are living. Follow your bliss and don't be afraid, and doors will open where you didn't know they were going to be."

More and more people are seeking a spiritual path that is more direct with the essence they call God than the path offered by organised religions. This is a personal preference, and one need not exclude the other. However, the word 'meditation' commonly replaces the word 'prayer.' Both traditional and 'New Age' paths are to be respected in recognising that we are all connected in the world of energy. Energy medicine, mindfulness and meditation have almost become buzz words. Whatever the practice becoming conscious of your true feelings it is necessary to go within yourself. To do this stillness is required and this can be achieved by stilling the mind with a meditation or mindfulness practice. You might like to state in your Advance Care directive that an environment which supports the chosen spiritual practice is needed.

Every thought and feeling has a vibration which has the potential to calm and reassure or to worsen a situation. Spirituality is the experience of the inner life. This direct experience of something greater can be sensed and transcends race, ethnic groups, culture, and tradition. Words like faith, grace, light, and guidance from the unseen world are expressed. A person's unconscious realm is known in meditation, altered states of consciousness, dreams, music, art, poetry and through those symbols and events push our buttons. For spiritual growth to occur, a person may evolve to recognize higher patterns of energy which some call archetypes, gods, angels, and spiritual guardians. It is about becoming self-aware through association with these patterns and character profiles that meaning is found.

Iain McGilchrist, the author of *The Master and His Emissary,* argues that the two halves of the brain have different functions. The right hemisphere is open, patient, empathetic, more interested in process than results. The left hemisphere sees detail, is precise, with an objective narrow focus. When working together they give clarity and precision, plus intuition and faith. They combine science and the arts and give facts and metaphor. However, not everyone seeks to dive deeply and for those who believe in reincarnation each lifetime is an opportunity for the personality or ego to grow closer to the soul.

   (a) This diagram demonstrates the conscious part of the self, the unconscious part of the self and what the Swiss psychologist CG Jung described as the collective unconscious. The collective unconscious is the field of energy where synchronicities and déjà vu occur. For example, the telephone rings and the recipient answers: "I was just thinking of you!"

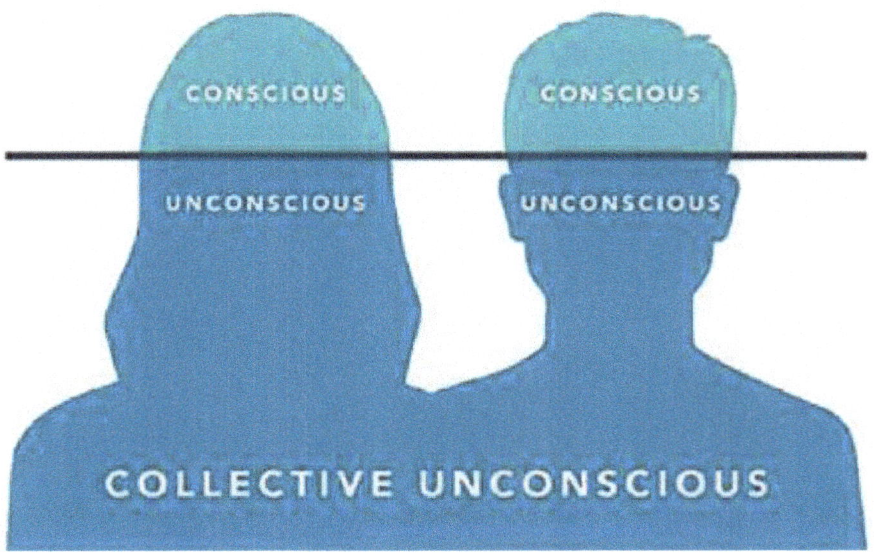

(b) This diagram demonstrates what some people refer to as 'the spiritual path.' It represents the journey from the ego which is all about 'I-ness' through that part of the psyche which is known through the five senses which relate to the tip of an iceberg. What is unconscious can be likened to the part of the iceberg that is below the water. This level of consciousness is reached with mindfulness and meditation, being aware of psychological projections and what 'pushes buttons.'

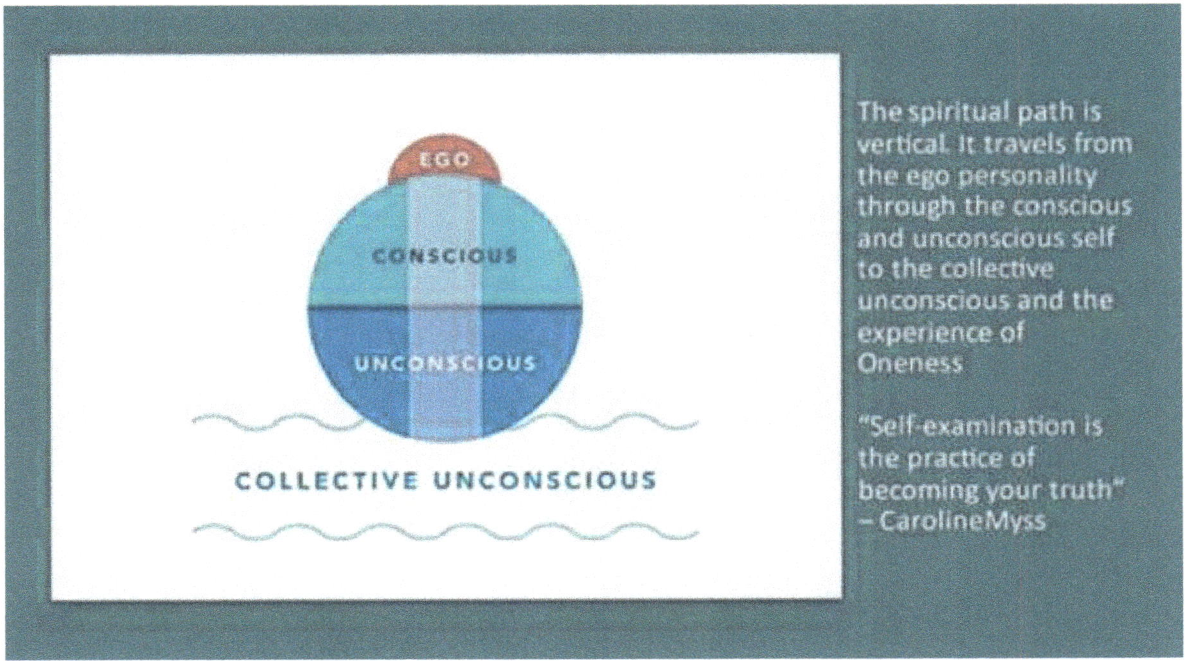

Plato called the collective unconscious the pool of ideas. Others call it the Akashic Records or the book of life or the angelic realm. Brian L. Weiss the psychiatrist who wrote the book, Many Lives, Many Masters teaches past-life therapy. I mention this to reinforce the soul as an energy that does not die at death. There is no need to fear death. This book begins with alerting the reader to the benefits of formulating an advance care directive. This is not a simple process as a person's world view is being made known. Life and death are one and when the fear of death is removed life can be lived in a fuller way.

I have referred to the ego as 'I-ness' and as the following diagram demonstrates it is the container a person builds in the first half of their life. Fr Richard Rohr, who is a contemporary Catholic priest, writes that in the second half of life a person fills the container with deeper ideas of life that considers what is best for everyone. While the ego likes to win at all costs, struggles to change others and the environment and fights for its share of power and control, the soul trusts that events unfold and seeks to transform by journeying inward and surrenders to a larger view of life.

(c) This diagram is an example.

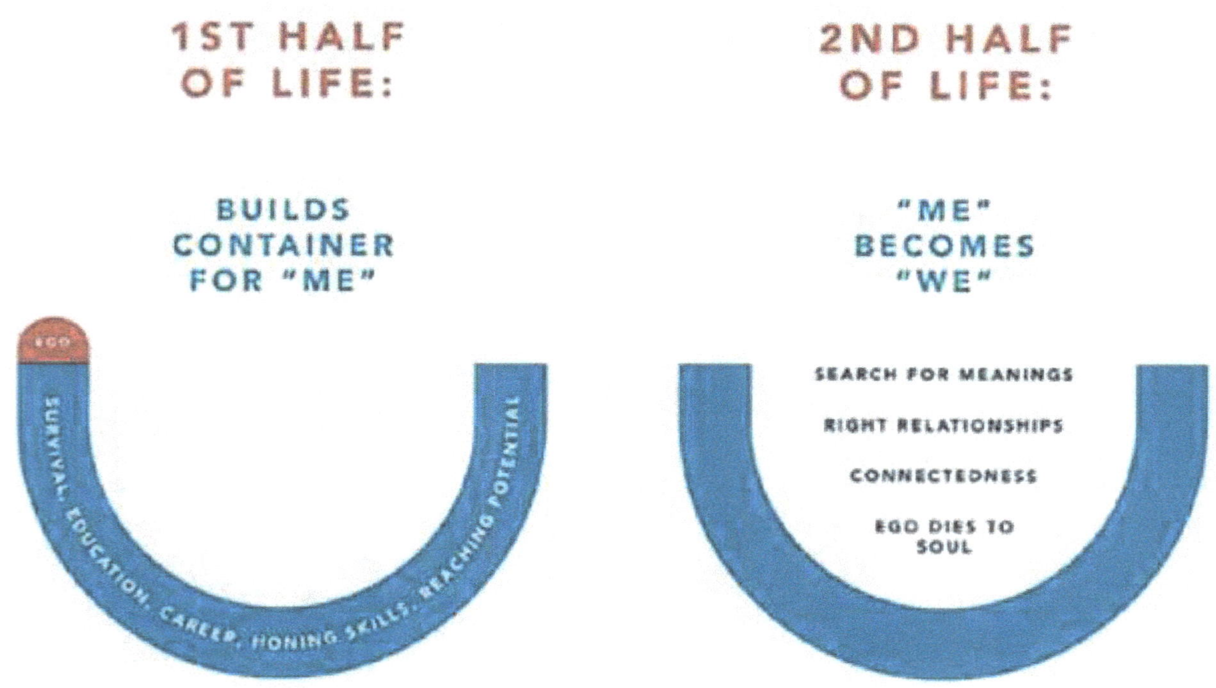

In the next diagram a person's needs has been divided into four quatrants and is based on the work of Dr Elisabeth Kubler-Ross the Swiss psychiatrist who taugh the world so much about dying.

Diagram of Holistic Care

Spiritual

Searching:
- for meaning in life/self
- for personal values/beliefs
- for trusting relationships

Practising:
- meditation/contemplation/ prayer
- living in present moment with love
- listening to/trusting intuition
- appreciation of nature/ natural order

Emotional

Experiencing:
- unconditional love
- forgiveness of self/others
- choice

Feeling:
- a sense of freedom/control
- the comfort of belonging
- a sense of usefulness / satisfaction / role
- the essence of realistic hope

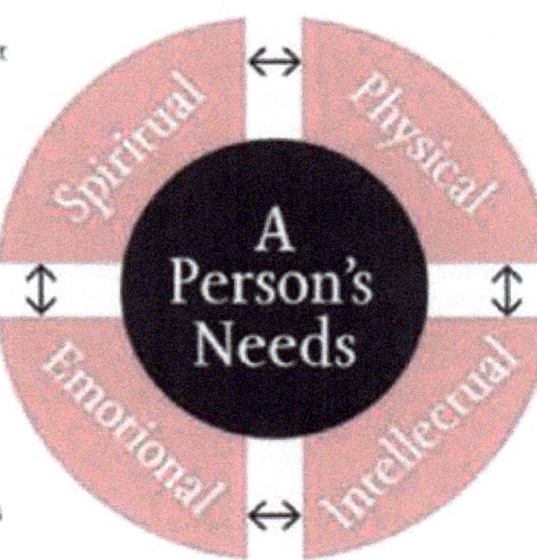

Physical

Obtaining:
- relief from troublesome symptoms
- appropriate nutrition
- bowel / bladder care

Experiencing:
- comfort/safety
- therapeutic touch/massage
- frequent hygiene
- periods of rest / activity

Intellectual

Obtaining:
- health information
- involvement in decision making
- effective communication

Understanding:
- benefits of positive approaches
- changes need not promote stress
- legal aspects of living
- funeral planning/ legacy

Life Review

With hints from our body that life is nearing the end it is common for a person to review their life. The following thought process may be helpful:

These things I have loved in life ....

....

....

....

These experiences I have cherished ....

....

....

....

These beliefs I have outgrown ....

....

....

....

These ideas have liberated me..

....

....

....

These convictions I have lived by ....

....

....

....

These insights I have arrived at ....

....

....

....

These risks I have taken ....

....

....

....

These sufferings have had silver linings ....

....

Life has taught me these lessons ....

....

....

....

These people have shaped my life ....

....

....

....

I have been inspired by these quotes and musical/stage performances ....

....

....

....

....

These things I regret ....

....

....

....

These are the achievements that give meaning ....

....

....

....

I sensed my life purpose to be ....

....

....

....

My 'unfinished business' is ....

....

....

....

My beliefs on life after death are ....

....

....

....

My beliefs on soul are ....

....

....

....

Therapies which have helped me find my inner self ....

....

....

Therapists who have encouraged self-healing and self-responsibility ....

....

....

 My spiritual life has these anchors ....

....

....

Listening to my body has influenced my health in these ways ....

....

....

I understand the role of energy in this way ....

....

....

I show love to myself in these ways ....

....

....

....

SECTION 2

A Most Important Decision – Where will you choose to live until you die?

Planning for the last years, months or days of life concerns everyone.

Dr Elisabeth Kubler-Ross wrote that people die in character. The following questions will help you to decide your character, values, wishes, and what is important to you regarding the place you spend this special time. You have more than physical needs. You also have intellectual, emotional, and spiritual needs – soul needs!

Questions to consider before leaving home or making a change.

1. Do you feel more secure in a known place?

    E.g., own bed, own garden, own view, own room, being with people you know.

2   Are you sentimental about the familiar?

    E.g., does the stain on the carpet or repainted veranda hold a special memory?

3. Do you value being able to make decisions?

    E.g., having a choice and ability or leaving an Advance Care Directive.

4. Do you rely on others to make important decisions on your behalf?

    E.g., your care team, doctor, religion, Substitute Decision Maker

5. Do you appreciate structure and routine?

    E.g., meals at the same time, a known care team.

6. Do you want to have a say in your care team?

    E.g., choose your own doctor, nurse or doula and times for care.

7. Are you confident in expressing your choices and making wishes known?

    E.g., do not want to make a fuss, churn inside when not understood.

8. Do you need to see tangible evidence of money spent?

    E.g., house, car, investment, or intangible spending like paying for care.

9.   Do you have a fear, rational or irrational, of running out of money?

    E.g., paying for health care, exceeding private health care benefits.

10. Do you feel guilty if you spend money on yourself?

    E.g., being able to provide for family more important than your own needs.

11. Would outsourcing the paying of accounts be helpful?

    E.g., this may mean that you can enjoy the time receiving care more freely.

12   Do you feel good when you put family and others first?

    E.g., find meaning in sacrifice. Agreeing to go into care to relieve family responsibility.

13. Do you enjoy meeting new people and fit in readily?

    E.g., find stimulation in conversation and new ways of looking at life.

14. Do you feel at home with your own age group?

    E.g., find it easier to share year-related life events rather than future.

15. Are you youth-focussed and enjoy passing on life skills and wisdom?

    E.g., appreciating the continuum of life and sharing knowledge and skills

16. Would you like more time to be reflective?

    E.g., appreciate a quiet environment and control over noise.

17. How have you coped with change in the past?

    E.g., see change as an opportunity and life as impermanent.

18. Are you finding responsibilities a burden?

    E.g., paperwork, bill to pay, appointments to remember.

19. Do you need to have a project?

    E.g., wood to carve, a jacket to knit, a book to read or a musical instrument to play.

20. Do you accept challenges?

    E.g., failing eyesight, hearing loss and decline in physical strength.

21. Are you comforted by nature and need a view of a garden, the sea and sky?

E.g., responding to the cycles of the seasons, feeling the flow of energy

22. Do you fear physical and emotional pain?

E.g., not receiving support and relief when it is needed.

23. Are you able to accept death as a natural part of life?

E.g., relax into another dimension when you feel it is your time or appreciate physician assisted dying.

24. Do you despair?

E.g., unable to make sense of a situation or express fears to a trusted person.

25. Are you comfortable when everyday events trigger a past memory?

E.g., forgiveness when needed is freeing, events in the past that need to be left behind can be put in a pink balloon filled with helium and released.

26. Have you discovered a source of faith and connection with the unseen world?

E.g., feel the need for a religious community or a quiet chat to a Pastoral Care person or appreciate a direct line with the Source or connection through a medium.

27. Do you hold grudges or project anger and confusion onto others?

E.g., the body is a gauge for emotional energy – sometimes loving and sometimes otherwise.

28. Can you let go of energy that does not relate to love?

E.g., Being peaceful and staying present in the NOW

29. Do you want to have a say in where you spend the last phase of your life?

E.g., Staying at home, moving into a care facility, hospice and perhaps sharing a room.

30. Do you need the ability to change your mind?

E.g., Experience a period of respite or have care at home.

31. Is it important to have your personal possessions around you?

E.g., favourite chair, bedside cabinet, bookcase, or TV.

32. Can modern technology support needs?

> E.g., Zoom connection with family and friends, iPad or YouTube entertainment, a buzzer to call for support or a sensor mat.

33. Is quality of life more important to you than quantity?

> E.g., live a full and active life even if it means taking risks.

34. Are health needs being met?

> E.g., prescribed medication is understood for its desired effect and possible side effects and alternative natural therapies are offered.

35. Do you want a say in your funeral arrangements?

> E.g., cremation or burial, private or public, clothing and memorabilia.

36. Have you attended to legal responsibilities?

> E.g., appointed an Enduring Power of Attorney and made a Will.

37. Are there charities you wish to support when you die?

> E.g., how do you wish to be remembered?

Whether it is home care or care in a health facility it is a choice for many. It is not a matter of right or wrong, preferred or not preferred. All have a valuable role to play. What is important is attitude, acceptance, and faith in what comes next.

Over my three decades of supporting people at the end of life I experienced cases where the final stage of life was brought to reality when the person made the move from the familiar to the unfamiliar as a way of acknowledging that it was time to put their affairs in order and to accept a time to face not being and able to go alone. This is the psychologist Erik Erikson's final stage of growth and the opposite of feeling a wasted and unfulfilled life.

For YOU and the care team

Practical Ways to make a person feel valued

Being encouraged to be themselves (warts and all)

- Inquire about major life events

- What was the biggest turning point in your life?

- What gives you a good feeling?

- What have you done in your life that made you proud and satisfied?

- What else would you like to do with your life?

- Where did you meet your life partner(s)?

- What upsets you about your life right now?

- When do you feel frustrated and angry?

Being listened to

- Receiving full attention

- "I said that I wanted one teaspoon of sugar in my tea"

- "I'm fine" (maybe I'm just saying it, but I don't really mean it)

- Having feelings validated

- Opportunities for gaining insight

- Hearing without judgement

- Noting descriptions of pain and discomfort

- Being given time

Having informed choices respected

- Refusal of medication or treatment

- Taking a risk

- Advance Care Directives

- Funeral arrangements

- Diet

- Exercise

- Daily activity

- Continence products

Having individual ways of doing things respected

- The arrangement of pillows or bedd ng

- The way the chair faces

- Where items are placed in the room

- Cutting fruit a particular way

- Covering particular parts of the bocy such as wearing a glove

- Day night reversal

- Having a night light or torch by the bed

- Brushing hair a certain way

Encouraging personal interests and giving feedback - eg.

- Your daughter said "what a patient person you have always been"

- Your grandson said "you made the best cookies"

- Your carer said that she just loves coming to you

- Your nurse tells me that you are a challenge!

- I can see you like watching the tennis on TV

- What book are you reading now?

- You have the loveliest hands – did you play the piano?

- Flirt a little

The Power of Choice

What choices does a person faced with a terminal or life limiting illness have?

1. They can choose to make decisions based on fear or based on knowledge and understanding

2. They can choose to heed the changes in their body or to ignore and deny them

3. They can choose to project or displace their deep fears - eg., fear of their own death may be expressed by talking about the deaths of other family members or other people, just as a child may say: "It's not my fault - he made me do it!"

4. They can choose their attitude and response - e.g., to find meaning or to despair

5. They can choose attachment or detachment to life as known

6. They can choose to make decisions based on natural therapies or based on a medical and scientific perspective

7. They can choose to be in the present moment – not thinking about the past or the future

A person's life is the result of the choices they make at the various stages of their life. A crisis is also an opportunity and a crisis like a diagnosis of cancer, may be a turning point that has the potential for a person to move forward or to regress. What may be viewed as mistakes can also be seen as lessons.

8. They can choose to make decisions based on fear or based on knowledge and understanding

9. They can choose to heed the changes in their body or to ignore and deny them

10. They can choose to project or displace their deep fears - eg., fear of their own death may be expressed by talking about the deaths of other family members or other people, just as a child may say: "It's not my fault - he made me do it!"

11. They can choose their attitude and response - eg., to find meaning or to despair

12. They can choose attachment or detachment to life as known

13. They can choose to make decisions based on personal values or based on a medical and scientific perspective

14. They can choose "knowing" and being "in the present moment" - acceptance rather than hope.

A person's life is the result of the choices he/she makes at the various stages of their life. A crisis is also an opportunity and a crisis like a diagnosis of cancer, may be a turning point that has the potential for a person to move forward or to regress. What may be viewed as mistakes can also be seen as lessons.

Fear acts as a negative magnet. What might they fear?

The unknown or future

Being out of control

Pain and suffering

Punishment in some form or karmic forces

Financial burdens

Abandonment by family, friends, and health professionals

Another Deeper Dive

My nurse practice was at the forefront of the spirituality revolution that is taking place in Western and Eastern societies, as politics and traditional religions fail to bring hope and meaning. There is a common cry when the question of religion is raised in a health Assessment: "I'm not religious but I'm a very spiritual person." On faith:

Faith can move mountains. What might a person have faith in?

- Signals from their body - if tired, rest; if hungry, eat a nourishing meal; if stressed, have a relaxing massage; if there is pain or another symptom, consult your doctor. Listen to the messages from the body.

- Sensing energy levels. Energy medicine is based on the chakras - found midline in the body. Chinese medical practitioners call it chi - to Hindu mystics, it is shakti. Subtle shifts in energy affect the cells of the body. Visualise and be familiar with your chakras - what parts of their body feel alive and what parts feel dull. Therapeutic Touch is a valuable tool for sensing energy.

- The power of the mind. The mind translates vibrations of energy into powerful images. Eg., butterflies in the stomach, weight on the head, a clenched fist in the gut, heavy heart, blocked arteries. The visualisation exercises from Neuro-Linguistic Programming are examples of using these images to gain insight into the body's signals.

- Comfort from a guardian angel, ancestors, God, love or karma. Inner guidance may draw a person to a workshop, to a particular doctor or healer. Guidance can come in meditation - quietening the mind. The mind might be telling us what our feelings and fears should be rather than letting our feelings and fears speak for themselves.

- Science. Evidenced based research assisted the doctor to eliminate 'trial and error'. Science and technology go hand in hand to minimise discomforts. Dame Cicely Saunders (2003), the founder of the modern hospice movement, demonstrated that hospice is a combination of heart and science.

- Dreams. Dr Judith Orloff, a practising psychiatrist and intuitive healer and the author of *Guide to Intuitive Healing and Second Sight* (2000) says that dreams keep a person well and provide the answers. She says that we are in partnership with our dreams and can dialogue with them. For her, dreaming is a direct line to a place where magic abounds, and nothing is without meaning.

- Meditation. Calm abiding or insight meditation. Calm abiding meditation allows the person to observe thoughts and emotions from afar - like clouds drifting past a clear bright sun in the sky. An example of insight meditation is stilling the mind to gain insight into the nature of the mind - a person's true nature.

My source of inspiration comes from Florence Nightingale who was encapsulated in my practice logo. Janet Macrae, US nurse researcher and Therapeutic Touch practitioner in her book *Suggestions for Thought*, reports that Nightingale did not abolish the concept of God, as she sought to unify science and religions in a way that would bring order, meaning and purpose to human life. Her great mind grappled with the most profound questions of human existence. Janet Macrae writes:

> *In 'Suggestions' for Thought, one has the opportunity to experience one of the great practical minds of modern history as it grapples with the most profound questions of human existence. As these basic human issues are universal and timeless, Nightingale's words are as immediate and compelling now as they were over a century ago.*

Putting heart and soul into care is a response from the core of each person who acknowledges healing and relationship as giving meaning to a lifetime.

Guidance

On Spirituality

Spirituality is the vital energy force that connects a person with the Universal Mind, or whatever name God is given, that has meaning for an individual person. It goes beyond religious affiliation and strives for a dynamic personal relationship with God. Common threads include: the search for meaning, the need to give and receive love and compassion, the need for forgiveness or letting go and the need for creativity and self- expression.

David Tacey is one of Australia's leading thinkers in religion and spirituality. He says:

> *To fall into spirituality is to fall into a larger pattern of reality, over which we have no control, and before which we stand astonished, mystified, and often disoriented. However, we do not fall into nothingness or emptiness; we fall into relationship with a secret or invisible other…*

Tacey believes that there is a need to move from the concept of the God 'out there' to the discovery of the God 'within'. He quotes Meister Eckhart who wrote in the 14th century, "*when God disappears from culture, we have to learn to give birth to God in the soul.*"

Sexuality and Spirituality

Sexuality is part of a person's life experience and frequently features in the life recall process and the struggle for self-development. Like spirituality, it is deeply personal and may shape a person's response to life. Religious psychiatrist Scott Peck, writing on the subject of sexuality and spirituality, says that according to myth, our sexuality arises out of a sense of incompleteness. He proposes that sexuality and spirituality arise out of the same need – yearning for lost wholeness and the search for God.

Stages of Spirituality

So how does spirituality relate to caring? People may learn to cope with and understand their suffering through the spiritual dimension of their lives. The more awareness a person has of their personal spiritual needs the richer a relationship can be. Small acts of kindness from a carer to the person receiving care can foster a relationship that is warm, genuine, and able to ignite a spark in the spirit of the person - this is spirituality in action. When I think of Peck's contribution to my understanding of spirituality I think about his valuable **Stages of Spirituality** which are described in his writings. They are:

Stage I - *Chaotic, Antisocial. In this most primitive stage people may appear either religious or secular, but either way, their belief system is profoundly superficial. It may be thought of as a stage of lawlessness.*

Stage II- Formal, Institutional. This is a stage of the letter of the law in which religious fundamentalists (meaning most religious people) are to be found.

Stage III - *Sceptic, Individual. Here is where the majority of secularists are situated. People in this stage are usually scientific-minded, rational, moral and humane. Their outlook is predominately materialistic. They tend to be not only sceptical of the spiritual but uninterested in anything that cannot be proven.*

Stage IV*- Mystical, Communal. In this most mature stage of religious development, which may be thought of as one of the spirit of the law, women and men are rational but do not make a fetish of rationalism. They have begun to doubt their own doubts. They feel deeply connected to an unseen order of things, although they cannot fully define it. They are comfortable with the mystery of the sacred.*

The Marriage of East and West

Bede Griffiths, a Benedictine monk, lived in the Saccidananda Ashram in India. He wrote of the Centre where all religions have their source and human existence its meaning. Saccidananda Ashram is a Christian community following the customs of a Hindu ashram and adapting itself to Hindu ways of life and thought. The ashram is a prayer-centre, where people of different religious traditions can meet together in an atmosphere of prayer and grow together towards that unity in Truth - the goal of all religions. I was privileged to spend a little time in this ashram with international author and spiritual scholar, Andrew Harvey in 2017.

Bede Griffiths writes that it is not any particular form of religion, but religion itself which is on trial in the modern world, and only an ecumenical movement among religions, each learning to accept and appreciate the truth and holiness to be found in the other religions, can answer the need of religion today.

A view in Bede Griffiths' writings is that Christianity shares with Judaism and Islam a Semitic structure of language and thought. His plea is that these Semitic structures need to see Semitic traditions with all their unique values in the light of the Oriental tradition - to learn what Hinduism, Buddhism, Taoism and Confucianism have to teach their tradition. This 'marriage' of East and West on a spiritual level will be the beginning of a new consciousness and answer the needs of the modern world.

People who are elderly and aware of their dying process can be wise teachers. When I said this to one elderly woman who was approaching death, she replied, *"I think you might be right."*

To be whole-hearted you must be happy…
To heal or to make joyous is therefore the same as
to integrate and to make one.

- A Course in Miracles

SECTION 3

Practical Tips

Physical Needs

- Is the bed comfortable, clean and dry?

- Is the patient comfortably clothed?

- Has the patient enough time for rest or activity?

- Has the patient enough to eat and drink? Is it the food of choice?

- Are troublesome physical symptoms being well managed?

- Is the patient in the environment of choice?

- Is the patient in the physical position of most comfort or choice?

- Would pampering treatments such as hot/cold towels be appreciated?

Is the bed comfortable, clean and dry?

An important consideration is to have a bed that is made with clean bedding and is well aired from time to time. Consider the possibilities of moving the patient to a chair or other bed (couch). For a bed to be aired, the room itself needs to be aired. Monitor the room temperature and make adjustments to the patient's clothing as necessary. The position of the bed can also bring comfort, if it is placed so that the patient can see some part of nature such as the sky, water and plants. Also of importance is that the bed is the one of choice - it may be that the patient feels most secure in their own bed. This may not be possible when considering the needs of the carers, and the occupational health and safety guideline to have the bed's height adjustable.

However, if a bed is not a suitable height, it may be possible to redesign the task in hand. Eg., instead of bending over the patient, is it possible to kneel down to perform the nursing task? Is it possible to use the 'Slippery Sam' lifting aid, kylie or woollen overlay to lift the patient while in bed? A double bed may be a nurse's nightmare but think of the comfort it gives when a loved one can lie beside the patient for intimacy. A larger bed also gives more room when there is a need to roll the patient for a change of position and bed making. Having a clean, dry bed helps to make a person feel comfortable and cared for.

Pay attention to the pillows. A favourite pillow in a clean pillowcase placed to give support to the head and neck, or several pillows placed to support the upper body can make the difference between relaxation and discomfort. The action of fluffing up pillows and turning them over is a basic nursing procedure and a ritual helpful in making the patient feel cared for. Fitted sheets are the best way for keeping the bedclothes wrinkle free. Loose plastic used as a 'draw sheet' is not recommended for protecting a bed as it easily creases and could harm the skin. Fitted protectors, air or water filled overlays and alternating pressure mattresses are less likely to cause harm to the skin and have the dual purpose of preventing damage from pressure.

Disposable continence products are practical and may preserve dignity and reduce laundry. When making a bed, it is important to notice if sheets are soiled with incontinence or stained with blood or crumpled in a way that indicates a restless time. These observations can help in assessing the physical needs of the patient.

Is the patient comfortably clothed?

Clothes are symbols, as well as practical items to keep a person warm and protected. Clothing needs to be clean and fresh. Clothes can also give a sense of continuing interest in life. E.g., bed socks or a head scarf may represent the colours of the favourite sporting team. A scarf can be added to serviceable bed attire to give a feeling of being dressed for an occasion. Leisure suits, kaftans and sarongs are practical wear when there are long periods of resting. Buttons may need to be replaced with zips or Velcro and garments may need to be opened down the back or made to fit loosely when dressing becomes difficult. Drawers and wardrobes are 'goldmines' for life recall and storytelling.

The task of tidying and sorting may establish which items are of sentimental value and which items can be passed on to a charity for recycling. Letting go of previously loved possessions is a step in the journey of detachment and evaluating one's values as well as kindling memories. The selection of clothes may also afford an opportunity to ascertain the garments to use after a person has died - often the patient themself has indicated a preference. A family member may wish to assist in the washing and dressing of a loved one following death. This is a culturally sensitive area and the care team need to check on customs and rituals before assuming responsibility.

Before washing and dressing the body after death, all nursing aids such as catheters and infusion lines are removed, and skin breaks sealed with an adhesive dressing. Clothes chosen at this time may include clean pyjamas, a particular nightdress or dress or suit that was worn for a special occasion. Being comfortable with discussions and preparations for death is a valuable step in the grieving process. Those who were present at the time of death will share a special bond with the bereaved. Being able to talk about the selection of clothes may provide a valuable link between living and preparing for death.

Has the patient enough time for rest or activity?

When one is sick or tired the body naturally seems to want to rest. It is important to create a serene peaceful environment free from intrusive noise and movement. Sometimes an elderly or very sick person needs to feel sad or disheartened and may withdraw from activity to be reflective and even grieve. This can be mistaken for depression. Sometimes there is day and night reversal when the patient seems to sleep all day and stay awake all night. Sometimes fear of being incontinent or being alone and helpless will disturb a natural sleep. It is important to provide a call bell, night light or a clock if time is important. Night-time is a natural time for dreams and reflection.

This presents the nurse or carer with opportunities to help the patient explore unconscious issues that may arise. It may be useful to encourage a patient to share their dreams and feelings. This may be a step in the healing of what Dr Elisabeth Kubler-Ross termed 'unfinished business' and used in her *Life, Death and Transition* Workshops (2001). Sleep can provide a temporary escape from physical and emotional pain, activities, and company. The doctor may order medication to provide sleep, but it is important for the care team to bring comfort by offering to wash face and hands, backs and feet. This may include massaging with a skin nourishing cream and applying a refreshing cologne or talcum powder. A warm milk drink and fluffed up pillows and adjustments to bedclothes may assist in the patient achieving restful sleep.

A reassuring manner assists in all areas of nursing care. However, if activity is desired, the activity needs to be patient-centred and be useful for stimulating the mind and imagination and/or exercising the body. A patient may not feel comfortable riding in a wheelchair but may be able to slide into a car seat for an outing and a breath of fresh air. Outings to a garden, the sea, the mountains, a previously lived-in house, a concert or movie may lift the spirit. 'Outings' may also need to be taken via the mind's eye by way of picture books, photographs and storytelling.

Has the patient enough to eat and drink? Is it the food of choice?

Food and fluids are more than body requirements. They may represent the food which was significant as a child or the food for special celebrations. They are a symbol of love and caring as well as a reward or distraction. The sharing of a box of chocolates or cup of tea can be a rewarding bond between the patient and those caring. It can make a patient feel special if the carer remembers little likes and dislikes. For example, how the person takes their tea or coffee and what fluid is favoured for the taking of medication. Special cups and utensils may be needed to compensate for a disability at meal times. Little touches of nature like flowers and herbs on a meal tray can delight. The patient needs to be asked with regard to the size of serving needed as they may feel guilty if food is not eaten although that is their preference. Mealtimes give structure to the day and can be reminders for medication. Having a choice is usually appreciated.

It is important to remember that our duty of care supports patient autonomy and sense of self, rather than imposing our view. Duty of care includes a duty to explain the treatment, possible alternatives, and the possible effects of consent or refusal. A patient who has a swallowing difficulty may be given a range of feeding options to consider. Withdrawing from food and fluid is part of the dying process. There are many papers written supporting the benefits of dehydration in the dying process. Care of the mouth is most important especially when the patient is no longer able to care for himself/herself. It is important to focus on quality of life for the patient rather than to encourage the patient to eat because that may make others feel good. Encourage the patient to listen to his/her body's needs. Ensure the needs of a patient from a different culture are respected. For example, the patient may not eat certain foods due to their beliefs.

Are troublesome physical symptoms being well managed?

Common physical symptoms include incontinence, constipation, nausea, vomiting and pain. Many of these symptoms are made worse by psychological factors. The mind, body and spirit are all connected. For example, fear may be a trigger for nausea or a feeling of not wanting to let go of control, which may manifest in the body as constipation. If a patient is unable to understand what is happening to them and there is poor communication, frustration may contribute to a headache or back pain. As members of the care team, it is important to look to simple ways of offering comfort and reassurance before requesting medication from the doctor. For example, nausea may be triggered by cooking smells or being served a large spicy meal. The art of caring looks at many factors that may be causing discomfort. Just a reassuring and calm presence can go a long way in making a patient more comfortable.

An accurate record and description of the patient's pain will assist the doctor in ordering the most effective medication, dose, and route. Part of the role of the care team is to be a patient advocate and to speak up for the patient – especially when he/she cannot speak for themselves. There may be times when they are unable to describe their discomfort or are too frightened to complain. There may be times when medications give more burdens than benefits and at all times the effects and side effects need to be recorded for the doctor.

Bowel and bladder management and their records are basic nursing responsibilities. Keeping a fluid balance record, temperature and blood pressure chart are not common practice in palliative care, as a palliative care focus does not support tests and records if the results are not going to improve the patient's comfort. The use of a dosette is encouraged when carers are required to administer prescribed medications. Some patients may choose to use herbal and other natural remedies. It is important that these do not react adversely with prescribed medications. This is a sensitive area, and often the faith in the natural product and the love and concern shown by family who recommend the product need to be balanced when assessing benefits.

Is the patient in the environment of choice?

This may be a hospital, nursing home or home itself. The need for special medical equipment and constant care may prevent a choice. Fear on the part of family may also prevent them taking the responsibility of caring for a very sick person at home. This is where the care team can play a major role by including the patient, family and friends in the 'unit of care' and offering supportive care and counselling. Care in the home may be ideal but it may be costly.

A sad situation occurs when an elderly or dying person has had time in hospital and is discharged to a nursing home without the opportunity to say 'goodbye' to their home and the memories of a lifetime. This is a loss and is followed by a grief reaction which may be mistaken for depression. Detaching from parts of life that are no longer useful is a process. Even a short visit to the former home with closure in mind can be powerful for healing. For some patients who are dying there is a need to leave home to begin to separate from this life. For other patients who are dying they feel most reassured and confident in their own bed for this major life event. It is important that hopes and desires are explored and put into place if possible. There may be a desire to return to a homeland, or to be buried or have ashes scattered in a place that had a significant meaning. In Asia, many are nursed at home by family members. One needs to be sensitive to and respect their specific needs.

Is the patient in the physical position of most comfort or choice?

Often a patient is most comfortable lying in one position and may be reluctant to change that position. If this was allowed to happen, a pressure sore is likely to develop as well as uncomfortable body stiffness. This is time to use technology such as an alternating air pressure mattress, medical woollen overlays or special foam overlays (like egg cartons in appearance). Arranging pillows can also be effective. In this instance the pillows are placed to support the body and leave a gap in the places where pressure would cause harm.

Pain relieving medication given prior to a move can make the process of moving less fearful and uncomfortable. It is difficult to put a time on the intervals between position changes as there are so many variables. For example, the patient may be soundly asleep and this may be more beneficial than relieving pressure. Having a mattress that changes pressure allows the patient to remain unharmed in the same position for long periods. Other factors include the general mobility of the patient, the weight of the patient and how close they are to death. If a person is close to death it is more important to have the continuity of loving company around the bed and nurture the spirit, even if it may be at the expense of pressure damage to the body. Performing passive exercises and massaging limbs to relieve stiffness and possible swelling may be a way the care team can bring added comfort to the bed-bound patient.

Would pampering treatments such as hot/cold towels be appreciated in addition to daily hygiene?

It has been said that cleanliness is next to godliness, and the use of water can cool, warm, soothe and comfort. Performing basic hygiene gives the nurse or carer the opportunity to observe the condition of the skin, hair and nails. Care of the hair and nails can make a difference in the way a patient feels about him/herself. Aromatherapy can be used alongside of hygiene and a few drops of essential oil in water can be used in many ways. Small face washers can be moistened, rolled up and kept in a plastic bag in a refrigerator for cooling, or they can be warmed in a microwave oven or immersed in a container of very hot water to have a warming effect.

There are commercial cloths pre-soaked in skin nutrients that may be used in the same way. Bath towels can be warmed in the sun, on a heating rail or tumbled in a clothes dryer to give a luxurious feeling. Soaking in a warm bath to which a bath gel and essence have been added affords relaxation as well as hygiene. Pampering treatments such as a head and neck massage can be included in a hair shampoo procedure. It is important for all clothes and towels to be clean and fresh. Using favourite powders and perfumes, shaving whiskers and applying face creams and makeup can help to promote a desired sense of self. A patient will remember the the care team by the way they made them feel.

Intellectual Needs

- Has the patient enough (or too much) information?

- Is the care plan understood?

- Is the patient able to communicate his/her needs?

- Is the patient involved in planning and decision making?

- Has the patient enough undisturbed time for reflection and thinking through issues?

- Would TV, radio, YouTube, reading materials be helpful?

- Would mental exercises, eg., relaxation strategies or reframing negative situations into something of a positive nature be helpful?

- Have financial, legal and ethical issues been addressed?

Has the patient enough (or too much) information?

In an era of Informed Consent (especially in Western medicine), there are many factors to consider when breaking 'bad news'. These include the age of the patient, the emotional intelligence of the patient, the desires of the patient and the wishes of the family and legal guardians. In many cultures it may be considered cruel to burden the patient with 'bad news', and it may be seen as a loving and caring act to keep knowledge of a condition that cannot be cured from the patient. The key is responsibility. Does the patient wish to be responsible for his/her own life and the decisions to be made concerning their life? Or does the patient trust others to make decisions on his/her behalf, believing that they will have his/her best interests at heart?

This is an area for much legal and ethical debate and there are no short answers. It is difficult for those responsible to know how much information to give – much medical and technical information may not be understood and merely confuse and frighten. Sometimes truth needs to be told gently and slowly. If the personality of the patient includes being an Extravert, the patient will need to talk about the news that he/she has been given. In a way they talk to think and by speaking the words they slowly make sense. An Introvert, on the other hand, will want to process the information internally and may wish to delay a conversation about what is understood.

Is the care plan understood?

The ideal is a partnership of care where the patient is the senior partner. It is too easy for the health team to formulate a plan of care as they see the patient's situation. Palliative care has at its core the need for care to be patient-centred. This means finding out the patient's goals, giving choices and encouraging the patient to make decisions within their knowledge. The plan of care may vary from a rehabilitation focus to comfort care or palliative care. For example, it may have been a lifetime wish to be rewarded at the end of working life by remaining in bed and being cared for during the last days.

Other patients may wish to die living life to the fullest and doing everything as near as possible to their known ways. Others may not have a choice and may need to change to another constant – eg., their mind and the way they adjust to the world. They may not be able to change the circumstances, but they may wish to change the way they view the circumstances. Sometimes what is perceived as a bad event can turn out to be beneficial in some way. Eg., a woman may say that when her husband died, she was devastated, but having to go to work has opened up a new world for her and made her self-sufficient. Goals need to be flexible and nurses and carers need to accept that the focus of care can change frequently and oscillate between realistic and unrealistic aspirations.

Is the patient able to communicate his/her needs?

Barriers may include language, illness such as stroke or brain tumour, or not being able to find the right words for expression of needs. The patient may be confused. A medication regime may need to be evaluated. Family members may be helpful, or it may be necessary to obtain the services of an interpreter. The language of loving touch can be a powerful way of communicating without words. This can be simply holding a hand or if the patient is very ill, placing a hand over the heart region while holding a hand (the heart/hand technique as taught in Therapeutic Touch). The technique of Therapeutic Touch taught by Professor Dolores Krieger and her colleague Dora Kunz is a valuable caring tool. This is a contemporary interpretation of several ancient healing practices and is being widely adopted by holistic nurses. Massaging pressure areas is basic good nursing care. Therapeutic massage such as a head, neck and shoulder massage is another way of communicating without words. It is important for nurses and carers to be aware of a patient's body language and document non-verbal signs of pain and discomfort. These may include frowning and rubbing areas of the body.

Is the patient involved in planning and decision-making?

This can be practised on very basic levels, such as asking if the patient wishes to receive care at a particular time or in a particular way. For example, asking what time food is to be served and what food would be welcomed. Planning may involve visits from family and friends and decisions may need to be made as to the length of the visit. Visiting is an area of great importance, and nurses and carers may need to monitor visits so that the visit is energising rather than exhausting. This may mean accepting periods of companionable silence, being involved in simple nursing tasks such as wiping a clammy brow or changing the position of a pillow. It is important for visitors to have an appreciation of the patient's condition and to give information such as snapshots of shared life, rather than ask questions such as "What does the doctor say?", "What have you had to eat today?". There may be situations when the decisions to be made are of a technical nature and beyond the understanding of the patient. A trusting doctor/patient relationship is essential. The nurse, carers or family members can all play an important role in speaking up for the patient when they are unable or not confident in doing so for themselves.

Has the patient enough undisturbed time for reflection and thinking through issues?

Patients often choose to stay awake during the night for reflective periods. This day/night reversal seems to bother those caring for the patient as they may wish to have the patient alert during the day, which seems more 'normal'. However when a patient is very ill or tired they may wish to 'escape' the business of daytime activities and sleep at that time. Family and carers can respect this process and it may be helpful to play soothing music for reflection or provide a night light for reading inspiring verses or favourite books. Too often medication is given for sleeping to meet perceived needs rather than needs that are patient-centred. If a patient is facing death there is often a period of anticipatory grief. During this time they realise and mourn the loss of everything known to them – the beauty of the earth, family and friends, material possessions that gave them a sense of accomplishments, and their health. An inner knowing of a terminal illness may exist – even if it is not consciously spoken about. These reflective times may be accompanied by tears, and if so the patient needs to have the privacy to cry rather than being given 'comfort' by a nurse or carer to stop the process.

Would TV, radio, videos, computer games or reading materials be helpful?

When holding a book or iPad takes up too much energy, the patient may appreciate a 'talking book'. There are libraries of books and poems available on the Internet to listen to and with personal earplugs if needed. Books with large print may also be appreciated. Picture books of nature scenes and paintings may be of interest as well as contributions of art and poetry from young children. Home videos of another era or favourite movies can be enjoyed and revive memories. Many patients find radio talk-back sessions comforting during what may seem like a long night. Also the nurses and carers need to be sensitive when there is a switch from favourite programs to silence. This can signal another stage in the journey.

Would mental exercises, e.g., relaxation strategies or reframing negative situations into something of a positive nature, be helpful?

Visualisation is the name given to a technique of helping a person bring a person or scene to their mind's eye. For example, if a person has some 'unfinished business' that is disrupting their peace of mind, that situation can be changed and healed. The situation may be that a valued person died without the opportunity to say "goodbye" or "I'm sorry". Imagination can help the person say what needs to be said or write a letter and in some symbolic way release what is causing concern. Visualisation can distract a busy mind and assist relaxation. This may be by describing a pleasant scene in nature or practising meditation. Often what seems like a disastrous event turns out merely to introduce another phase of life. Visualising the healing effect of medicine or treatments has recorded benefits.

Have financial, legal and ethical issues been addressed?

It is not uncommon for practical affairs to be avoided. The making of a Will may be seen as a sign of giving in. Family may not wish to ask about these matters as it may be seen as grasping for inheritance. It has traditionally been the role of a man to be the provider for the family and if his life is in danger, or if dementia limits his rational planning, an extra burden is placed on remaining members of the family if details of assets (insurance policies, bank accounts) are not known. Cost of treatment versus benefit may cause an ethical dilemma. A patient may refuse treatment if he/she perceives the cost detrimental to his family. On the other hand a family may spend resources on unrealistic treatments that do not add to the quality of life for the patient or prolong life. Emotional states are frequently not rational and early planning has many benefits. The ethical dilemma of 'truth telling' plays a major role in making 'end-of- life decisions'. Having a meeting of all members of the unit of care and care team can often facilitate the way forward.

Emotional Needs

- Is the patient able to feel useful and needed?

- Does the patient feel that he/she has 'unfinished business' (e.g. forgiveness of self/others or unresolved grief)?

- Is the patient being validated as a person (correct name/title)?

- Have the patient's accomplishments in life been honoured?

- Does the patient feel loved (without conditions)?

- Does the patient feel free to make choices?

- Have emotions such as fear, guilt or remorse been addressed?

- Does the patient have a sense of belonging to a family, group or country?

Feelings of self-worth can be encouraged by highlighting and affirming the ways the patient has touched the lives of others. This may be simply by being an inspiration or a catalyst to bring the family together. Most patients at the end of their life due to disease or old age like to feel that their life has had some meaning or purpose. Carers who attend a patient's funeral are often surprised to learn the achievements of the person they knew merely as an old man who wet his bed and had to be fed. It may be appropriate for nurses and carers to ask family members to share the person's personal journey with them. Writing the Personal Introduction section of the Assessment can be a practical way of learning about the patient's contribution to the lives of others. It is also an opportunity to show what the nurse has observed. Eg., "I can see that you are a very private person who has worked hard and had a commitment to making improvements in your personal world." "You have a very supportive family and now maybe the lesson is for you to accept care from others." "You have had many setbacks, but you have a fighting spirit." "What a lot of things you have achieved."

Does the patient feel that he/she has 'unfinished business' (e.g., forgiveness of self/others or unresolved grief)?

Dying is like coming to the end of a journey. It is a time for reflection – regrets, unlived lives, achievements, insight, and trust in a higher power or life force. It can give peace of mind if perceived 'wrongs' are put to acceptable 'rights' if possible. There may be a child who was sent away for some reason. There may be errors in honesty. There may be doubts, fears and guilt about any number of matters. A flash of life review is commonly reported by those people who have had a 'near-death experience'. It is important for nurses and carers to be non-judgemental. Empathy is the key – trying to put oneself in the other person's situation. It is not possible to know what another person is feeling. Humanist psychologist, Carl Rogers believed that value is achieved when a carer gives unconditional positive regard, real caring and acceptance. He said it was important for the carer to be genuine and to give attention to love, creativity, joy and "peak experiences." For this sort of caring the nurse or carer needs to appreciate that they bring their own prejudices, values and self-acceptance with them when they are with a patient.

Is the patient being validated as a person (correct name/title)?

It is important to think of patients as more than people who have a particular diagnosis. It is important to show respect by calling the person by a formal title (Mr or Mrs), unless invited to do otherwise. Calling an older person by a first name may make them feel uncomfortable and not respected. Nurses and carers are privileged to enter into the home of a person and especially so in a caring role. Everyone has different ways and familiar ways of living. Sensitivity is needed to establish the unit of care's known ways of living before assuming a teaching role or projecting personal ways onto another person. It may be appropriate to admire the sporting trophies, the travel mementoes and children's contribution to the atmosphere in the sick person's home.

Have the patient's accomplishments in life been honoured?

This aspect of a person's life is more than achieving wealth and possessions. It includes character, survival, inspiration and ways in which the person's life touched on others. Perhaps the greater accomplishment is the realisation of the Self and its potential. The Humanist psychologist Abraham Maslow demonstrated people's aspirations by a triangular diagram.

At the base of the triangle are listed the basic physiological needs such as clean air and water, adequate food, sleep and warmth. Then comes safety factors such as protection from physical and psychological injury, safe environment, trusting relationships. Ascending the triangle Maslow documents the need for belongingness and love. This includes the need to be connected to a family, group or country. It includes experiencing the warmth of loving touch and actions and being taken seriously and being heard. (A person feels important if they are listened to.)

Following comes self-esteem which includes being validated as a person, receiving recognition from others for achievements and experiencing feelings of freedom and confidence. On top of self-esteem is self-actualisation, and this represents the journey through life and reaching potential. That may include developing skills and competencies and taking risks. At the top of Maslow's triangle is the desire to know and understand, and aesthetic needs. These needs include the need to search for meaning in life, seeing the overall picture of life and things done, things loved, and beliefs formed. Aesthetic needs include feelings of oneness with the universe, bliss, delight in nature, art and music and above all the skill of 'living in the moment' and accepting mystery.

Does the patient feel loved (without conditions)?

Dr Elisabeth Kubler-Ross in her writings frequently refers to the need for nurses and carers to give love and care without conditions. This means caring without expecting praise and "thank you". This means being able to care for angry, manipulative and even abusive patients in a manner that says: "I am here for you – I understand that you are hurting inside and 'dumping' on me those unconscious hurts". It is important that nurses and carers do not respond in protest but rather with a statement that acknowledges the patient's feelings. E.g., "When you are angry, I feel sad and incompetent – how can I make a difference to the way you feel?" If a patient's outbursts are taken personally by the care team, then they need to look into their own lives to see what is hidden in their own personality.

Often the skilful use of humour can change the atmosphere. The humanist Carl Rogers believed that if caring stems from the helper's own need of being liked and appreciated, constructive change is inhibited. Co-dependence is another word to describe an unhelpful caring relationship. E.g., A nurse's or carer's self-worth is dependent on the patient needing him/her. They are compulsive helpers and place conditions on their care – they need to be needed and appreciated. There is a danger of 'burn-out' for this type of nurse or carer. To look after others effectively, the nurse or carer must first be able to look after themselves. This comes with self-knowledge and awareness.

Does the patient feel free to make choices?

This relates to 'breaking bad news', Informed Consent and completing an Advance Care Directive. It requires a trusting relationship. There is no such thing as a silly question when a patient or member of the unit of care is trying to make sense of a situation. Often patients may not ask a question for fear that it will expose their lack of knowledge. Patients may be heard to say: "I feel out of control", "I'm helpless", "It's all my fault", "I feel scared and uncertain". It may help to explore some of their thoughts – thoughts are not feelings and are not facts. By changing thoughts and feelings a choice to improve relationships can be presented. It may be useful to help the person reflect on what was happening when they became upset and write down what they thought and felt. It may help to look for facts, the effects from thinking and feeling in a certain way. What choice of thinking and/or feeling is going to be most helpful in the situation?

Have emotions such as fears, guilt or remorse been addressed?

To do this nurses and carers may need to listen to the telling of life stories - over and over sometimes, as the person tries to make sense of an occurrence. By listening creatively, a person's feelings of being able to solve their own problems are fostered - this leads to a sense of worth, purpose and understanding. It is especially important to listen to what is not being said - what is behind the masks and manners. Hidden fears may include the fear of taking morphine, the manner of death, being left alone or rejected. It is important to realise that the most important gift we give to people is ourselves.

Often it is our fears and prejudices that become projected onto those in our care. E.g., if the patient is suffering from breast cancer and the nurse's or carer's mother died from breast cancer, there is a risk that the mother's way of managing her disease may be recommended or otherwise to the person currently receiving care. If there is a desire to make amends, meetings may be facilitated. Often these feelings are associated with grief and are normal grief reactions. One grief may trigger the memory of another grief that was unresolved. E.g., the death of a husband may bring back memories of the death of a father or even a much loved pet animal.

Does the patient have a sense of belonging to a family, group or country?

Issues that arise here are often issues of 'homeland' and being connected. Patients may belong to cancer support groups and associations for their particular illness. There are support groups for particular losses – e.g., support for people who have experienced a death in their family. Belonging is one of the needs identified by Maslow. The need to belong is seen in the divisions between cultures and creeds. It carries feelings of approval and acceptance. A person's personality will also be a factor in determining this need. For example, a person who receives their energy by interacting with many people will need more social interaction than a person who is energised by being alone and interacts with few people.

A caring organisation such as a hospital, nursing home or hospice can give people a sense of belonging when length of stay permits. If care is seamless in an organisation and allows for different stages of a person's life and illness, a sense of belonging is achieved. For example, the aged care complex that caters for independent living, nursing home and hospice care. Nurses and carers also need to have a sense of belonging. This may be to their employing organisation, to a stable family unit or religious or other group. Within an organisation there is the need for a team approach when all members need to have an appreciation for each other's differences in skills. Successful teams need a leader. The Myers-Briggs Typology Indicator is useful in helping team members to understand themselves and how they function in a group setting. E.g., some personalities will focus on data collected by the senses and impersonal analysis. Other personalities will focus on what might be, rather than what is, and make decisions based on values.

Spiritual Needs

- Nurses and carers need to be aware of the significance of spirituality.

- The patient may feel a loss of belief in their God ('dark night of the soul')

- A love of life or sense of oneness with all things may be missing

- The patient may need to feel 'at peace' with God and the world

- The patient may feel that his/her life is incomplete

- The patient may lack in confidence in 'Letting Go'

- There may be frightening dreams or intuitive apprehension

- Does the patient's life have meaning? A sense of the spirit within?

- Is there a feeling or acceptance of the divine plan or continuation?

The patient may feel a loss of belief in their God ('dark night of the soul')

'The dark night of the soul' is a term used by mystical writers to describe the despair a person feels when the faith they thought they had deserts them. There is no firm 'handle' to hold onto. Buddhist leader, Sogyal Rinpoche in his book *The Tibetan Book of Living and Dying* writes:

> *One of the chief reasons we have so much anguish and difficulty facing death is that we ignore the truth of impermanence. We so desperately want everything to continue as it is that we have to believe that things will always stay the same. But this is only make-believe… impermanence is like some of the people we meet in life – difficult and disturbing at first, but on deeper acquaintance far friendlier and less unnerving than we could imagine.*

When health is altered and life circumstances change, there is often an anger expressed at God rather than an acceptance of God's will. The person feels that faith in a God has let them down. Feelings of loss are a prelude to grief and in order to gain spiritual insight a person may go through a loss of some kind. This loss may be a loss of health, the death of someone close, a loss of relationship, a loss of function, a loss of dreams or a loss of possessions. Grief offers the opportunity for the unconscious to permeate the conscious. Too often an interesting job, a beautiful house, material wealth and a comfortable lifestyle divert a person from inner fulfilment. When loss occurs the person may feel that there is nothing to hang on to for security. All the things that helped previously do not help in the present situation.

A love of life or sense of oneness with all things may be missing

There are many paths towards fulfilling spiritual needs and it is not the role of nurses or carers to prescribe any particular pathway. For many their path will be a particular religion or philosophy but there will also be patients who value spirituality as a force that helps them to understand the universe and laws of nature. Talking about nature is usually a universally accepted way of meeting spiritual needs. The seasons of the year, night and day, morning and evening, sunrise and sunset are all symbols of change. A beautiful flower or plant has a life cycle as do insects, animals and birds. For some a person's soul may be seen as a droplet detaching from an ego state that defines them in this world, to join the vast ocean of life. For some there will be a belief in a heaven and a hell state. For others there will be a belief in reincarnation. Sadly, many people neglect to look for their particular path until a tragedy like a terminal illness occurs. I see people who die with a love of life as having a good death.

The patient may need to feel 'at peace' with God and the world

The setting in which the patient is nursed will contribute to feelings of peace. It is important for it to be clean and tidy with symbols of strength and reassurance in view. These symbols will vary. E.g., they may represent religious objects, statues of gods, flowers and miniature waterfalls, cards and letters from family and friends, photographs, and sporting trophies. Silence may be appreciated, or music may be helpful in calming the senses. Nurses, carers and visitors need to be sensitive to preserving the atmosphere in a patient's room and for cleaning and respecting the chosen symbols. Nurses and carers need to feel comfortable with asking about spiritual issues – just as they do with asking about physical, intellectual and emotional needs. Peace for some may follow the visit from a religious figurehead. They may need to receive forgiveness for times when they felt they 'missed the mark' in a particular action. The care team may ask the questions: "What else would you like to do while you still have strength?" "What will give you a sense of peace?" "How do you wish to spend your energy today?"

The patient may feel that his/her life is incomplete

This feeling may relate to age or to a life project. Incomplete suggests something is not whole – that is why holistic care that strives to consider the whole person is important. Feelings of incompleteness can arise in different areas of a person's life. It may be there is a need for relationship. It may mean that there is a need for greater insight into the Self. Jung's theory is defined by bringing into balance the opposite functions, desires, thoughts etc. that are part of the person. These will be conscious and unconscious. It does not mean eliminating the opposites but accepting the opposites and owning every part of the person, including the 'shadow'.

For many it seems that there is a soul journey, and although it may be painful doing the things that we least prefer, it is a way of bringing the opposites to a middle path. For example, a person who is an extraverted feeler may benefit from using introverted thinking. When thinking about the word 'incomplete' it is important to remember the grief experienced by the people left behind. Nurses and carers guided by the Nurse-in-charge may wish to attend the funeral or send a card or flowers as a token of remembrance. Anniversaries and special dates like birthdays are often difficult times for the bereaved.

The patient may lack confidence in 'Letting Go'

For those who walk beside a dying patient there is often a point when the patient seems to 'let go' of the struggle to live. There seems to be a struggle with ego and a survival gene that surfaces in the dying process. The patient may consciously express a wish to die but there seems to be an unconscious desire to stay alive. There may be fears for the survival and coping skills of family members. There may be frightening dreams or intuitive apprehension. When a person is close to death they often describe people who have died before them and see what they describe as angels. Being punished for sins and the justification in being wounded or ill may be felt by some as necessary for the change from a materialistic selfish world to one of self-sacrifice and the quest for authentic living. Dreams are the interface between this world and the next.

This period of care is often marked with what is described as 'terminal restlessness' and sedation may be helpful for the patient, family and carers in the vigil. Lasting memories are formed at this time and the sight of a loved one plucking at the bedclothes and moving in distressed confusion can be haunting. From a spiritual perspective, it seems that during this time the soul or psyche is struggling with an unresolved issue. It is a belief that nature attempts to heal the psyche just as it does the physical body when it is injured, and as this is an unconscious process the administration of sedation can be reassuring to those in the vigil. Death is neither hastened nor postponed and many nurses who care for dying patients will say that the patient dies when they are ready. It is most important to respect the dying process and the feelings of those in the vigil. Tears are a normal process and nurses and carers need to be comfortable with a person who is crying and not try to bring a crying episode to closure.

There may be frightening dreams or intuitive apprehension

Sometimes medications seem to have an adverse effect and the patient may hallucinate and see ants and spiders. Other patients report that they 'see' or feel the presence of ancestors or angels. This may be a time when the person who is dying experiences 'the dark night of the soul' as described above. Having company may be invaluable to bring comfort and reassurance. If medication is suspected of contributing to the experience, this needs to be reported immediately to the doctor. Some spiritual traditions warn that a person may face their own 'demons' of fear, anger and mistrust. Peace may be restored if these 'demons' are acknowledged and released. It is important for a patient to be reassured and encouraged to forgive himself/herself for whatever feeling that may arise. Different religious traditions have various ways of releasing uncomfortable feelings. This may be by confession to a priest or praying special prayers or receiving sacraments.

Does the patient's life have meaning? A sense of the spirit within?

The search for meaning is a lifetime quest for many people. A person may ask themselves what the purpose of their life is – and even question if there is a purpose. Spirituality is associated with meaning. It is associated with relationships - relationship with oneself, relationship with others and relationship with God or a world view. There is a need to accept the reality of the loss and change in whatever way fits into a person's beliefs about themselves, the seen and the unseen world and the universe. If these beliefs and faiths are not securely grounded, there can be a loss of faith and disillusionment rather than an inner strength.

Love and compassion are universal threads of all major religions and faiths. Prayer and meditation are tools used by many people to connect with the God within. Art and music are also tools. They provide a symbolic language by which the unconscious speaks to the conscious self. A person may watch a movie, or be touched by a poem or a chapter in a book in a special way. Feelings that surface may be sad or happy. E.g., a person became very sad and frightened during a storm. It was not the storm itself that caused the feelings, but it was a reminder of the stormy night when her husband was killed. When people experience grief, they may regress to a former state in their life when they felt safe and were coping. This may even be to the time when they were a child.

Is there a feeling and acceptance of a divine plan or continuation?

Is there life after death? Or does the patient believe in 'dust to dust' – no more? Is death fate? Is it preordained? If a patient is secure in a belief, they will more easily reach the stage of loss described by Dr Elisabeth Kubler-Ross as 'acceptance'. For some, there is a belief in a soul that lives forever and continues to develop towards good or evil, following the direction it has commenced on earth. That is, the soul retains all traits of personality and psychic functions and travels on the energy particles that left the body at the time of death. For some there is a belief that a soul can choose a rebirth for the purpose of learning lessons and so gaining enlightenment. Christian, Muslim, Jewish, Buddhism and Hindu faiths all teach a life after death.

Care of a Person at the Time of Death

Pre and Post-Death care is significant for many reasons:

- it is a time for withdrawing and reflecting - the world narrowing down to simple things

- it is an opportunity for inspirational example: "I'm dying but I'm doing it well"

- it is a time for saying goodbye - loving so much that the personal loss is outweighed by a desire to see suffering and struggle ended

- it is a time for showing love and commitment - staying by the bedside, encouraging visitors to promote life recall - including the person who is dying, but avoiding demanding, exhausting responses from them

- it is a time for reassurance and encouraging an attitude which acknowledges a love for life and acceptance of death as a part of life - rather than "poor me" or "why me?"

- it is a spiritual time - a time for seeking understanding - in life and in suffering – for finding comfort in a belief or God, seeing how the illness is bringing the family together or giving an opportunity to address issues of a spiritual nature

- the clock cannot be put back - no regrets or unsaid good-byes - the family and friends may wish to be present at the moment of death and when this occurs disappointment may be expressed - a comfort to some is a belief that the dying person chose the moment of death or letting go

- the dying person may be like a frightened child and need comforting, stroking, handholding, and hugging by people who are accepting of the dying process

- people may die as they have lived and although the struggle may take many turns, described by Dr Elisabeth Kubler-Ross as the stages of dying, medical interventions need to be wise - medications may be used to ease noisy breathing (Death Rattle) and changing breathing patterns may need to be explained

- attending to legal concerns – such as an Advance Care Directive, Enduring Power of Attorney and a Will

- funeral arrangements need to be anticipated or confirmed - the Soul Talks' Funeral Planning booklet may be helpful.

- washing the body is a mark of respect which some loved ones like to share - it is helpful to choose ahead of time the clothes to wear at this time or to give to the funeral director

- viewing the body can be very helpful in reassuring that suffering has ended and the soul energy has left the 'shell'. Medical equipment and personal possessions give way to fresh linen, flowers and meaningful mementos

- staying with the dead person while waiting for the transfer is a time for reminiscences

- including an article in the coffin can be symbolic - the portable radio or Ipad that never left the side in life, the card with a child's drawing, the letter saying the things that were felt but not able to be said

A word of caution

Cultural and religious influences will play a major role in the rituals and spiritual support given to a person who is dying, and in caring for the body after death.

Sometimes you may be tempted to preach to the dying, or to give them your own spiritual formula. Avoid this temptation absolutely, especially when you suspect that it is not what the dying person wants! No one wishes to be "rescued" with someone else's beliefs. Remember your task is not to convert anyone to anything, but to help the person in front of you get in touch with his or her own strength, confidence, faith, and spirituality, whatever that might be. Of course, if the person is really open to spiritual matters, and really wants to know what you think about them, don't hold back either.

Sogyal Rinpoche

Section 4

Belief in an Afterlife

People who have experienced the presence of a departed soul no longer doubt that there is an afterlife.

Grieving people's lives are changed following these communications and there is the realisation that death is a continuation and not a permanent separation.

Communication comes in different ways to those who are sensitive and intuitive, such as mediums. Messages are received in different ways. For example:

- Sensing a presence in a room

- Hearing a voice when there is no one near

- Smelling a perfume that a significant message

- Seeing a loved one

- Feeling a touch

- In dreams and via symbols

These messages are not hallucinations. Many books have been written about connections with the afterlife but there are still people who are afraid to share their experiences for fear of being thought irrational. Symbols are the language of the soul and speak more clearly than words.

Dr Cherie Sutherland, who has had a near-death experience herself, was a Visiting Research Fellow in the School of Sociology at the University of New South Wales. She has written many books on the near- death experience. She compared stories from her research and noted the similarities which gave her a better understanding of the phenomenon.

One story gave this insight:

> *We are all a part of God, we are immersed in spirit…Each of us is like a cell in the body of God, so we all have God's inherent qualities: love, peace, wisdom etc, but we don't recognise it because we have this sense of separation.*

Raymond Moody in his book "The Last Laugh" writes about near-death experiences, apparitions, and the paranormal. Dr Moody is the author of the ground-breaking book "Life after Life." In "The Last Laugh" Dr Moody refers to the word *fey* to describe an unrecognised paranormal phenomenon that frequently occurs among those who are about to die. This otherworldly word has meaning to many nurses and hospice workers. Dr Moody writes: *"From personal experience at the bedside of the dying, however, I know that the phenomenon exists and is fairly common."* He believes that the reason that close observation of the dying process is less observed is the trend for people to die in hospitals rather than at home. Medical practices frequently obscure paranormal events at the time of death.

Near-death experiences are also reported over a wide expanse of time. For instance, Plato wrote in The Republic in 450BC about Er, a Greek soldier killed in battle, who, twelve days later, after reviving on the funeral pyre, went on to describe the journey his soul had taken during this time. And in the vision of the sixth century saint Salvius of Albi (recorded by Gregory of Tours in 590) we are told his soul rose from his lifeless body, accompanied 'to the height of heaven' by two angels. Salvius described entering the other world: being brought through 'a gate that was brighter than our light' into a place where the floor shone and there was an ineffable light that was indescribably vast.

Anecdotal Examples and Commentary

Looking back upon my experience as a registered nurse specialising in palliative care, there have been many opportunities to share a close relationship with a person who is dying, and to form a relationship with their family and friends. 'Walking the journey' with a person who is dying requires comprehensive insight and assessment. While medications assist the patient's mind to free itself from the discomforts the physical body may be experiencing, a comforting presence may go a long way in providing emotional support. Kind words may give reassurance, and expressions of love will support the spirit.

The first death I would like to share with you is that of a person I will call Charles, who was in his eighties and dying of cancer. He was supported by a very caring wife and two children. He cheekily called his wife his "Brown Sugar" – sweet but needing a little refining. He was a staunch churchgoer and felt secure in his Christian faith. As he entered the final stage of his illness, he received opioids for pain relief and a small dose of sedative. He was being nursed in his chosen room in his own home. This gave him a sense of security and protection.

One day I was giving him a massage, and in a calm voice, I was taking him through a visualisation, with images that incorporated the colours of the rainbow. I invited him to be a feather on the breath of God (his language and the words of Hildegard of Bingen - medieval nun and author). His wife was holding his hand. The whole atmosphere in the room was peaceful and calm. As the massage continued, his breathing became slower and slower. I tried to match it, while continuing with the imagery. I thought this was a wonderful way to die. Suddenly Charles opened his eyes and said: "I can't do it – I'll have a cup of tea!" I responded with a smile: "Would you like porridge too?" It was an incredible moment. Here was a man trying to die consciously. I felt like a midwife to the soul. One day I left him with Cheyne-Stokes breathing, and carefully monitored my pager for a call, which did not come. When I returned, he was sitting up in bed with all his family around him. He had awoken and summoned them. He said that he had seen the glory of God and wanted to give them all a blessing. He did in fact die several days later, but only after sharing what he was "seeing".

It has been said that the wisest people in the world are the people who are dying and who know it. Rather than fearing and hiding from death, new insights can be gained by those who sit at the bedside of a dying person. This reminds me of an elderly woman who was dying from cancer. She said that her family was upset with the diagnosis, but she wasn't. She was pleased to be in her own bed at home and was content to look back on her life and her many achievements. I had spent several nights with her, and on this particular night, I informed her that I wasn't able to be with her anymore, as I was going away. Her response stays with me: "That's all right, Joy – we have met many times before and we will meet again." I told her that Elisabeth Kubler-Ross says that people who are dying are the wisest people on earth. To this she replied: "I think you may be right."

Working with the breath, as in mindfulness, is helpful for many people who are entering the dying process. I have been inspired by the Tibetan Buddhist tradition. At a workshop for Phowa practice (transference of consciousness) I learned about a technique that can be used by people of all faiths and religions. The patient is encouraged to imagine a narrow hollow tube connecting the region of the heart and the top of the head. Inside the tube is a pearl, which represents the patient's essence or soul. With every breath, this pearl rises and falls. While this is happening, the tube ending at the crown is opening. The person invites their God (from whichever spiritual practice), when it is time, to harvest their pearl through this opening. Comforting words in the Christian tradition are those Jesus said on the cross: "Not my will, but Thine, be done."

Physical comfort can be given by moistening the mouth and creaming the lips. Jumbo swabs or foam swabs are useful. Water with a soluble gel is all that is needed. I recommend a Lanolin product for the lips. It is helpful to have the patient nursed on an air-filled alternating pressure mattress and medical woollen 'drawsheet' so that there is no need to disturb the person who is preparing for death. I encourage those at the bedside to massage the patient gently with a lavender cream and to hold a hand. Face washers soaked in water, to which an essence such as eucalyptus has been added, can be rolled and stored in the refrigerator, and later used to wipe hot and sweaty skin. I usually sprinkle lavender essence on the pillows. There may be a smell of impending death, and it is important to use aromatherapy to override this.

Many patients and their families have expressed fears of there being a mistake when death has been pronounced. Once death has occurred, I find that it is helpful to involve a family member or other person who was close to the deceased, in the preparation of the person's body. This not only brings a sense of reality, but it is also a vital step in the grieving process.

Emotions are not necessarily rational, and even health professionals are often in need of support and explanation when confronted with strong feelings. An example of this occurred with the death of a patient, whose wife was a nurse. The man had just died from cancer at a rather young age, and his wife had a fear of a deep coma state being mistaken for death. By inviting her to help in the washing of her husband's body, she was able to see the pooling of the blood in his back when he was turned over. She could see with her own eyes that the heart was no longer circulating his blood. Together we washed and dressed her husband in clean pyjamas and tidied the room, ready for the children to spend some time with their father. Acknowledging that death had occurred and a life change had begun were the first steps in her grieving process.

The moment of death is very special, and relatives will often want to be present. How can a nurse recognise the signs of approaching death? Doyle writes:

> *All colour drains from the lips, the eyes immediately lose their lustre and moisture, breathing stops, the pulse in the neck is no longer seen and a deep peace descends – a peace which, for all that it is real, is difficult to describe.*

The pulse is certainly a significant sign that death is imminent. Contrary to what many lay people think, rather than slowing, the pulse becomes rapid and shallow near the time of death. When death is expected, the person's breathing becomes very shallow and irregular and those present may wonder if each breath is to be the last. The breathing may also be noisy, as secretions collect at the back of the throat - this is normal and may respond to medication being given subcutaneously. Suction is not advised, as this tends to cause distress. The patient's eyes may roll back as they do in deep meditation. Those at the bedside appreciate an explanation of what is happening and what is normal.

When those waiting for the moment of death are not able to be present, it may be a comfort for them to think that the person has some control over the time of death. I will say that sometimes the patient's spirit or energy is held by the energy of those around them, and for the spirit to leave, this energy needs to be absent. In the Buddhist tradition, we are told that the subtle mind - the essence of the person - expands, and there seems to be an ability to connect telepathically. Rinpoche says that the clairvoyant consciousness of the dead person in the bardo of becoming is seven times clearer than in life. This can bring them *either great suffering or great benefit.*

I reassure those who were not able to be present that if they were thinking about the dying person, they were indeed connected. For those who sit in the vigil, there is often a desire to help the person to make the transition. Sometimes the patient actually needs permission and encouragement. Thoughts at this time may include: "let go", "focus on feelings of love", "feel good about yourself", "let the balloon go", "go to the light". I tell the patient to think of a situation when they felt love – be that the moment of a birth, or a wondrous sight in nature, or feelings for a spouse. If it seems appropriate, I say that God is love, and that by holding love in the heart, God is also there.

The process of grieving begins long before death and I find that by being present at the time of death to share that special moment, a trusting bond has already been formed.

On the practical side: Note the time when breathing ceased. A doctor will be needed to certify death. In the community setting, I establish if the regular doctor wishes to be notified should death occur at night, or if he/she would rather be notified in the early part of the morning. Sometimes the family doctor advises that a locum doctor is to be called. It is wise to be supported and have regular visits from the family doctor for legal as well as health reasons.

When there is an established relationship between the doctor and nurse, I begin preparing the body for family viewing and the important vigil period. Preparations include straightening the body, replacing any full or partial dentures (sometimes these are ill-fitting, but by closing the mouth, the facial form is restored), and closing the eyes (this sometimes requires a moist film of cotton wool or tissue to be placed under the eyelid). Urinary drainage catheters and subcutaneous lines or cannula, are removed if present. Medical equipment such as oxygen masks, mouth care trays and air mattresses need to be removed. Broken skin is sealed with an occlusive dressing. An all in one incontinence pad is positioned to secure any leakage from the bowel or bladder. A man may need to be shaved. Hair may need to be shampooed and dried and finger nails manicured.

So that the hands can be held, they may lie on top of the bedclothes, either beside the person or across their body. A thin cake of soap or the inside the cardboard tube of a toilet roll, or a long lipstick case wrapped in a handkerchief or scarf, are useful for propping the jaw in a closed position. There is no need to cover the face, and often, as the tension disappears, the person looks very peaceful and 'special'.

Candle or dim lighting seems appropriate. Those present may wish to sit for a time beside the bed with their reflections and feelings. For some, grief may be too acute to appreciate staying by the bedside and this is acceptable too - they may prefer to go for a walk, or to take solace with another person, or visit a favourite place. Flowers can be arranged in the room or on the pillow. Music can be played if desired by the family. A favourite memento or verse may be placed with the person who has just died. Jewellery is usually removed, but some people express a wish to be buried or cremated with a sentimental item. Others will act as the father of two young children did, when he put his children on the bed to see that mummy wasn't breathing any more. He symbolically removed his wife's rings and said to the children: " We will keep these as a memory of her."

Choosing how to dress the person who has just died is important and again it is helpful to involve the family. For a patient who was a grandmother, I experienced a touching moment when her eight-year-old grandson asked if he could help after his grandmother had died. I asked him to choose a nightdress, which he gave to his mother to iron. As I prepared to wash his grandmother's body he asked me: "Why are you doing that?" A little taken aback, I replied: "Out of respect for the house she lived in." When she was lying peacefully in state in her own bedroom, with the bed covered by the bedspread that matched the curtains she had made, I asked the husband and daughter when they would like me to arrange the transfer to the funeral home. The husband, who initially wasn't keen to accept the responsibility of having his wife at home, changed his mind, and wanted to keep her for the night. The little boy put his teddy bear on the chair beside her – to keep her company! At the funeral he was there dressed in a bow tie, holding the attendance book for all to sign. He looked very proud and I'm sure will have a reassured approach to death in the future.

Asking the dying person about what clothes they would like to be dressed in is an opportunity to enforce the reality of death and to explore preferences and symbols. For example, one woman wanted to be clothed in the dress she had bought for her daughter's wedding. It was her celebration dress and she chose this symbol for her own important life event. Dr Richard Lamerton says that whatever one believes, all great teachers have accepted that the dying must prepare for another world. Never should this preparation be interfered with. It is helped by simple qualities such as goodness and beauty, with which we should surround the dying. Sometimes it is appropriate to say a prayer or to have a quiet moment around the bed - for example, reciting the Lord's Prayer or just saying something spontaneous like: "You died well.", "There is a feeling of love and light" or "Thank you for being you". Reading a poem or inspiring verse, playing recorded music such as the music of Chants from Taize (a spiritual centre in France run by Protestant monks) or just holding hands, can often express feelings when no words can be found. It is important to ask those at the bedside if anyone needs to be contacted and given the opportunity to say "goodbye." This may include a leader from a spiritual tradition or a person who supported the family by caring for the garden or house.

Depending on circumstances, it often aids the grieving process if the body is not hurried away. Funeral people will come at any time, although there is usually an extra charge for 'out of hours'. The process of grieving, expressions of love, and goodbyes are helped by the vision of a body that is not suffering and is peaceful - a shell. Valuable time can be spent 'viewing' or being with the body. I saw an example of this benefit when a husband, father and grandfather died in his home at the age of ninety. It was a timely death that occurred in the early hours of the morning. The wife who suffers from dementia was sleeping in a twin bed in the same room. The daughter, who had personality issues with her father, was present at the time of death and willingly helped me with washing and dressing her father's body. It was very much a healing time for the strained relationship. The man's wife watched the procedure from her bed and asked questions (often the same question) from time to time.

The family doctor advised that he would call in the morning to certify death. It was decided to ask the funeral people to come in the evening, as that would allow two daughters to travel to say their good-byes in the privacy of the home. Grandchildren (teenagers) came throughout the day and experienced their first view of death. They sat on their grandmother's bed and talked about their grandfather and what they would remember about him. It was all very natural. I believe that it was my role to help dispel this anxiety surrounding death. In this case, the daughters arrived and all the family and the nurse shared a meal. Following the meal, which was really a celebration of family life, there were photographs taken of the family including the dead grandfather. For them this was a family event and they entered into the spirit of farewelling this man who had provided well for them. It seemed that the wife who suffered from dementia 'forgot' about the death during the day, but when the funeral people came, she stepped forward as head of the family to take them into the room where her dead husband lay. She could touch him and feel that he was cold. This realisation helped her to accept that he had left her.

Some other personal experiences include a widow who kept her husband's body in the bed next to her all night, saying: "I knew he wasn't there, but I just wanted him for one more night - I let him go in the morning." A fourteen-year-old girl tied her friendship bracelet around her father's wrist. Confessions, acknowledgments, tears and fears are expressed at this time. Those who die from a disease process are seen to be free from suffering and that helps the feelings of loss and love.

After the funeral people have transferred the body, the bed needs be stripped, leaving the room with an acknowledgment of change and 'knowing'. Medications prescribed for the person who has died need to be destroyed safely with the permission of those responsible for handling the deceased's affairs. The family may wish to be spared the transfer of the body to the funeral vehicle, so that their last memory is of their loved one looking at peace in the bed where the final goodbye was said.

Those present may appreciate help with telephoning the news to family and friends and making practical arrangements, such as notices for the newspaper, writing the obituary, and organising accommodation for travellers to the funeral. Those left behind may want solitude, or a walk on the beach, company to share a cup of tea, or to have a drink and reminisce. Some may just want to sleep - especially after a long vigil. Not everyone will accept this level of involvement with a person who has died and that is when the funeral people have a role to plan.

A continuum of palliative care nursing for nurses and carers is to attend the funeral if appropriate. I have found that it is common for family to be touched by this action, which in reality, is a way of debriefing and saying thank you for the opportunity to gain further insights into death and how best to offer comfort and empathy. The funeral service can be one way of celebrating the person's life, as well as a means of helping the bereaved. Remember that each person is an individual and that what is right for one person may not be right for another. For some it is useful to plan the funeral before it is needed. This involves special honesty and acknowledgment and is rewarded by knowing that the person's life was marked by an event that was personally meaningful. One example of this was at a home funeral - as the coffin was leaving the house a racing pigeon was released. It circled the house before returning to its home. (As well as being symbolic, racing pigeons had played a part in the man's life.)

As a first step towards 'walking the journey' with a person who is dying and the 'unit of care' (patient, family and friends), health professionals need to address their own conscious and unconscious issues about death. An unconscious anxiety regarding death can so easily be projected onto another person.

The unconscious communicates through symbolic language. It may be by a dream, or a feeling that is roused when we look at a cross, a country's flag, or a painting. It may be when we hear a particular sound, like the sea or a piece of music. It has been said that art and music are the language of the soul. Flames may be a symbol of purification, while the snake is the traditional symbol of healing. Fairy tales are full of symbolic language. Many people see cancer itself is a symbol - a symbol of death and decay, something to be feared. Sports heroes and actors have become symbols. For many, Princess Diana was a symbol, representing the struggle of life, the disappointments, betrayal, hope, service to others, caring, motherhood, beauty and humanity.

We can never give away that which we ourselves do not have. If we are fearful and uncomfortable at the death bed, those we are trying to assist will feel this. In the words of social worker and counsellor John Ashfield:

> Our capacity to genuinely help others is almost directly proportional to the extent to which we stand on 'solid ground' within ourselves - ie. the extent to which we accept and are comfortable with who we are.

Corey, Carl Rogers and Abraham Maslow, major spokesmen for humanistic psychology, suggest the following principles to bring about adjustment and change for patients:

- Give attention to love, creativity, joy, and "peak experiences" – aesthetic needs

- Focus on the person rather than the problem – "how can I become myself?"

- The therapists themselves must be genuine – not phoney professionals

- Establish a therapeutic relationship based on empathetic understanding

- Give unconditional positive regard, real caring and acceptance

Carl Rogers believed that if caring stems from the helper's own need to be liked and appreciated, constructive change or knowledge of the self is inhibited. It is important for the helper to enter into, and identify with, the patient's private world, without losing the separateness of their own identity.

We need to be familiar with grief and what is a normal grieving process. We need to appreciate what the Bible describes as "the seen and the unseen" in life. Many people who are dying have sense and sight of another reality. Patients have said things like: "Are you still on this side?" "There is a man here who knows about that." (as I talked about going to a lecture on Neurolinguistic Programming to a visitor); "I can see my black dog"; "It is all an illusion." To my mind it is indeed a privilege to be present at these times. Near- death nursing care is much more than caring for the physical body.

Bereavement Care

All professionals involved with care of a person with terminal illness need to consider their role in the support of family and friends following the patient's death. Each culture has its own ways of managing grief, its own rituals, its own understanding about what happens after death, its own rules about how to manage death ceremonies appropriately. In a multi-cultural setting, it is important to respect the particular needs of a family at this time.

Grief is a common accompaniment of loss, particularly the permanent loss of a loved companion, and it is known to be a cause of significant distress and physical symptoms, and to contribute to a worsening of other health problems, to suicide and to death itself.

Grief may be prominent during the course of the terminal illness - anticipatory grief; it may occur as a crisis of distress around the time of death - acute grief; or it may surface in other forms, including depression, months or years after the time of death.

Grief is a multi-dimensional syndrome, which includes anger, guilt, anxiety, irritability, sadness and a decreased ability to perform usual tasks. There may be physical symptoms such as anorexia, sleep disturbances, fatigue, headache, palpitations, and hair loss. Common emotional consequences include a feeling of helplessness, apathy, numbness or denial. Grief can be classed as complicated if the affected individual fails to return to pre-loss levels of performance and well-being, but this situation can be difficult to recognize as sufferers will often try to hide their distress, feeling perhaps that they "should have got over it".

The process of making progress through and out of the trough of grief has no set pattern or timing, but will usually include:

- A recognition of the reality of loss. This may be facilitated by gentle prompting: *"Tell me about your partner's death".*

- Awareness that things have changed: *"How are you different"?*

- A willingness to recollect and re-experience the relationship: *"Tell me about your husband/ wife".*

- A willingness to consider letting go of old attachments: *"What do you feel has changed since he/she died?"*

- A readjustment to that change, and a willingness to look to a new future: *"What do you think the future holds for you?"*

Some individuals become 'stuck' in their bereavement: They remain focussed on the loss, express bitterness or anger that it happened, are unable to find pleasure in distractions, seem unwilling to let go of their grief. If there is clear evidence of vegetative effects of depression - poor memory, restless and sleepless nights, loss of appetite – anti-depressants may be considered, but it is probably even more important to facilitate open expression of the hurt being experienced. If the bereaved person will join in a group to meet others who understand, this may be more important than drugs. Do not suggest that it will soon pass - grief is a process to work through, and that work may take a very long time. But it is appropriate to assure such a person that it will not last forever.

I have endeavoured to be mindful of the traditional values and beliefs of Eastern and Western societies. In this context bowing to feelings of loss and acknowledging the grieving process may seem inappropriate when God's will is a fundamental belief governing a person's religious faith. Personal feelings may seem an indulgence in the light of God's plan for a person. Some Asian cultures may place a higher importance in restraining from showing emotions in the interest of maintaining harmonious relationships which support the greater good.

However, having an understanding of bereavement and mourning assists in the understanding of other life events and processes and allows a person, regardless of culture, to be more fully present with those who are experiencing a loss and dealing with that loss in whatever way is appropriate for them.

During our life we are often confronted with feelings of loss and grief. Some of these losses can be small losses, such as when we leave our parents and go to school. Other losses can include divorce or the death of a loved one.

Pain and suffering come with attachment and if a person is able to experience the pain of loss during a lifetime and then move on, they may approach death more easily. Therefore, it is important for those who are caring for people who are dying to have an appreciation of the person and the ways they have coped with loss during their lifetime. To do that we first need to understand the significance of loss in our own lives and develop personal ways of growing through that loss and its associated feelings. This book invites the care team to evaluate their own understanding of grief and loss. The more we are able to nurture ourselves and experience and express our feelings, the more we will be able to accompany others as they journey through loss and grief.

Grief needs to be shared

During a time of grief, a lot of respect is needed, because people grieve at different levels and at different times. You cannot make an appointment with grief; it just happens when something triggers feelings in you. The death of a loved one affects our lifestyle and changes our self-image. Grief can rapidly shape us and help us to discover a new independence and outlook on things. This is expressed in many ways. Grief is a growth process. *Grief needs to be expressed - the pain we feel needs to have meaning.*

Ways of dealing with loss:

1. Acknowledge the loss and share with someone who will validate the feelings associated with loss and show empathy. Mention the person by name.

2. Allow the feelings to come without trying to push them back. They may be sad or hurt feelings, anger and resentment or relief. Write about them and then watch as flames consume the writing as a mark of release.

3. Cry if you feel like it. Be with someone who will not try to comfort you or stop the flow of tears. Tears contain endorphins and provide natural healing.

4. Share thoughts and concerns and remember that emotions are not rational, they are just emotions.

5. Recognise any personal or learned behaviour that may get in the way of the grief process. Knowing your personality type may help in this area. Religious beliefs and cultural norms may assist or form barriers.

6. Look for the lesson in the experience.

7. Deal with unfinished business such as forgiveness of self and others.

8. Write down wishes and desires that cannot be changed and find a way to release them. You may wish to burn the piece of paper or throw torn bits into the wind or sea. You may wish to visualise them floating off in a big balloon. You may wish to take a mindful walk and release unproductive thoughts, feelings, and concerns with every step.

9. Say or write an affirmation and repeat it each day until the hurt diminishes.

10. Remember the Serenity Prayer: *God grant me the serenity to accept the things I cannot change, the courage to change the things I can, and the wisdom to know the difference.*

11. You may wish to perform a ritual such as lighting a candle that is personally meaningful to you or you may wish to visit a particular place to connect with nature or your God.

Pre and post death considerations

For thirty years I sat at the bedside of people who were dying. Some of those people were extremely fearful while others were profoundly peaceful. During those years I would encourage relatives and those in the vigil to be present for those last breaths. Present in physical form and present as in the 'present moment' or the profound NOW as described by Eckhart Tolle. Witnessing the energy leave the no longer needed physical body, is a profound moment not to be feared or avoided. It is learning about dying. From Teresa of Avila translation: "The Beloved looks less at the grandeur of our deeds than at the love with which we perform them." This is the gold standard for all those at the bedside of a person who is dying – professionals and non-professionals! Ramana Maharshi who was able to transcend the boundaries of the body, senses and mind said: "I am not the perishable body but the eternal Self."

As a palliative care nurse, I would recommend and strive to achieve a calm, loving and respectful energy at the bedside. This can be difficult in the presence of fear, overactive minds, busyness accompanied by noise and money worries. To eliminate these distractions is most helpful to the person who is dying. The environment plays a complementary part. A clean, tidy room filled with fresh flowers and with a view of trees, sky or mountains produces its own calming energy. Softly playing music and/or chanting mantras or prayers also has a calming effect. However, all is personal, and preferences need to be established by consultation. What is an affront to the senses for one person may be welcomed by another? This guide contains suggestions from my nurse practice.

There are three relationships to consider when striving for a peaceful state of consciousness in preparation for death. The first is the relationship a person has with themselves and the quality and vibration of the energy generated from their thoughts and emotions. Thoughts tend to be fuelled by emotions. For example, the emotion of jealousy can fuel a range of thoughts. Then there is the relationship a person has with others. Different energy vibrations affect each other as seen with two tuning forks – when one is set to vibrate the second one also vibrates. Thirdly, there is the relationship with the energy vibrations of the unseen world. Achieving the highest vibration in these three relationships requires awareness and work over a lifetime. In my practice years I was aware that I could only accompany a person on the spiritual journey as I far as my personal journey into awareness and consciousness had taken me.

> The body can live without food easier than the soul can live without meaning – Shakespeare, Macbeth, Act 5, Scene 5

Involving the Children

A much-loved grandma had been discharged from an acute care hospital to her home to die. Her eight- year-old grandson had ridden in the ambulance with her, helped to settle her in bed and expressed the wish to watch the nurse insert a urinary drainage catheter to afford the comfort of a dry bed. He held the torch and accepted the explanation that grandma now had a bladder outside of her body. When she died he still wanted to be involved and chose the nightdress, picked flowers from the garden and wanted to know why the nurse was washing his grandmother's body. The nurse replied: "Out of respect for the house she lived in while she was alive". When the room was made straight with the matching bedspread which grandma had made, he placed his teddy bear on the chair beside her - so that she wouldn't be lonely until the funeral people came next morning. At the funeral he presented himself, complete with bow tie, to record the names of all those attending the funeral.

Another much loved grandmother was gently dying in her hostel room. The grandchildren came to visit and stay for a period of the vigil. The family dog came too and entertained the nurse and family by doing his commando tricks in respectful silence. The youngest child sat on the floor with the Scrabble set and connected letters to spell out: "I LOVE GRANNY". Tears flowed and events which gave examples of granny's kindness were affirmed. Granny quietly and gently stopped breathing soon after they left the room.

A young mother had just died, her children aged two and four. The father encouraged them to climb up onto the bed and see that mother wasn't breathing anymore and emphasised that they could now climb on the bed and be near mummy without their movements causing her fearful pain. The father removed the rings from their mother's finger and said: "We will keep these as a reminder." They all kissed her goodbye.

Four teenage daughters were standing beside the podium at their father's funeral - each remembering their relationship with their father in different ways. The youngest turned to the coffin and said: "And we are on time!" Another teenage daughter took off her friendship bracelet and tied it around her dead father's wrist - cementing their relationship. She had only got up to take her part in the funeral because her name was on the programme - but returned to her seat bursting with pride.

Conscious Dying

"I don't want you to talk to the doctor about my vomiting because I'm not going to eat any more - it won't be a problem." This man was lying in his bed at home and being cared for by his wife who confirmed that he was a man to stick by his decisions. He and his nurse shared a description of what his dying might involve. The conversation included a description of physical symptoms

Marie Curie who won the Nobel Prize twice for her pioneering work on radioactivity said: "Nothing in life is to be feared, merely understood." My patient just wanted to understand what he was experiencing.

Charles was a man of great character and firmly believed in God. His pathway to God had been via the Anglican Church. He was not afraid to die and rejected hospital treatment for pain. He acknowledged his good life and just wanted to get on with dying and meeting his God. I was taking him through a massage/meditation session, relating the colours of the rainbow to plants and flowers in his garden and suggesting that he become like a feather on the breath of God. His wife was holding his hand in thoughtful farewell. This peaceful scene was interrupted by: "I can't do it. I'll have a cup of tea!" We all had a chuckle. This was the first of several practices for dying - other times he appeared near death only to regain consciousness and summon the family for blessings as he had seen the glory of God and wished to give them all a blessing from his personal experience.

Laura was a dramatic little lady whose curled and carefully positioned hair framed her painted face. The mirror to check her appearance was under the pillow. She had had a long battle with cancer and having prepared her husband, was content to die with the aroma of her much-loved rose garden wafting in through her window. Three days before she died, she peacefully told me that she was halfway across the river Styx. She died as she wished - with her two sons present waiting for a breath that didn't come.

Another lady whose death was just days away picked up from the carpet an autumn leaf turning brown. I asked: "Do you feel like that leaf?" Our eyes met in confirmation.

"Are you looking forward to your one hundredth birthday?" I asked a strong woman. "Oh, it depends on how hot the summer is," was a reply which indicated acceptance and reflected a previously stated "I'm content to wait for the chopper to fall". "I've made the doctor promise that he won't let anyone take me away unless he is sure I am dead." As she was dying, she said: "My feet are getting heavy - I want to be carried upstairs". As a child her bedroom had been upstairs, and it was as though she was asking to be carried to rest.

Similar sentiments were heard expressed by an elderly gentleman who requested his mother to lift him out of the water.

Saying Goodbye

One-night Joan, at the age of fifty was preparing to die. There had been prayers with her daughter, blessings from the priest and recorded messages for absent friends and relatives. Joan roused suddenly and asked me: "Who is coming in the morning?" - indicating that she had postponed the event.

"He died on my birthday and our son's birthday - and it was the greatest gift he could give me". This wife had great difficulty in saying goodbye because her husband had always been the decision maker and she took comfort in consulting with him. "I just hope that he is on the ceiling with our birthday balloons looking down on us. I won't ask him to make any more decisions."

Thoughts of going home and reflecting on symbols of home are frequent at the time of death and may be ways to encourage a release from the struggle. Geoff, a man in his forties, was encouraged by his wife to: "Let the balloon go. Don't keep Mollie (Mother) waiting with her Sunday roast."

Music may play a part in letting go: a famous statesman expressed the wish to say goodbye with the great church music ringing in his ears; a woman who was a determined fighter stopped breathing dramatically when the music changed from soothing relaxation music to a short stimulating piece of music entitled "Lean on Me", which had been specially written for her during her illness by her son-in-law.

Giving out communication signals which convey comfort with the dying process encourages questions such as: "Am I dying?" These questions can be answered with a squeeze of the hand, a kiss on the forehead or an honest "Yes". I felt compelled to answer this question by confirming that the patient had left his world in order, his mortgage was paid, his wife was looked after. The reply from the dying man was: "I got the message."

Relatives may be reluctant to say 'goodbye' because they fear that this might evoke magical thinking and precipitate the event. Often the dying person continues the struggle in response to "I'll see you tomorrow, Dad." Another goodbye might be: "I know that this is an effort for you and the end is coming – you are much loved and if you choose to die in the night so be it – if you decide there is more to do I will see you tomorrow!"

Grace always considered others and was the organiser. Her brother in his eulogy said: "Grace took three days to die so that she could help us with our grieving."

Ways which Encourage Positive Feelings and Honour Love

David was only in his fifties when he died. He had been a popular sportsman, farmer, good citizen, much loved father and husband. In the week that he lay dying he had eighty visitors. Brothers-in-law and good mates sat around the bed drinking beer and remembering, often with humour, various life events. The reminiscences were not intended to exclude David, who every now and then raised his hand to interject on a point.

Another man remarked: "I'm only sixty but I've lived eighty years - playing A-grade cricket, golf and bowls as well as working hard."

A little lady with a southern European background was dying and over fifty members of the family came to visit. She acknowledged them all with a blink. As her breathing became more and more shallow, her husband and sons reminisced about her work and community achievements. The sons recalled how she had cooked breakfast for their football mates and put up with them playing soccer with balls of socks in the corridor. She would have heard how her life of being wife and mother was appreciated.

Often during a long vigil, it is helpful to record the salient points of the life in readiness for the funeral people. This adds a focus to what is taking place and often affirms the struggles, disappointments, achievements, and relationships. "I always liked her in her red dress - I think she should be dressed in it - I'll show you the photo of the last time she wore it."

"I believe in miracles." Encouraging realistic hope, removing fears, and looking for meaning, even in disappointments can be a challenge. Obviously, there are situations where it is difficult to seek positives, and the miracles and feelings of self-worth seem to be happening to the people around the person who is dying, rather than to the person who is dying. Changes to a present direction may be made with the realisation that death is so final. These questions often arise: What do I value? What do I want to leave behind? How do I wish to be remembered?

Five Strengths for Death Preparation – A Buddhist Perspective

The following five strengths for death preparation is inspired by the teachings of Tibetan Dzigar Kongtrul Rinpoche who is the author of the books, *It's Up to You* and *Light Comes Through*.

1. **The strength of honesty and good deeds – a life lived by being true to yourself.** Now is the time to let go of your attachments, to let go of accumulated assets and worldly matters, which only serve to cause suffering at the time of death. Pain and suffering come with attachment and when considering a lifetime of accumulating only suffering and despair will accompany a mind that is still connected with tangible assets and their future. Prepare a Will and consider giving to a charitable cause as well as considering the real needs of your family.

2. **The power of meditation, mantras and bodhicitta.** In Buddhism, bodhicitta is the mind that strives toward becoming more conscious and aware. It shows empathy and compassion for the benefit of all life. It vibrates at a high frequency. To acquire this state of mind a person may benefit from finding a teacher or community from various traditions - an inward path to follow! This strength includes the soul's journey and the intention for positive karma to ripen and a sense of oneness with the universe and all life.

3. **The strength of critical intelligence.** This is being aware that all feelings such as fear, loss, confusion, anger, and despair. These are expressions of clinging to the needs of the ego. The ego self needs to be released for peace to be experienced. By clinging to these feelings there is a danger that they will consume the mind at the time of death. The best preparation to avoid suffering and anguish is to consciously prepare for death while there

is time. There is a realisation that a lifetime has purpose and meaning, and happiness is the goal.

4. **The strength of setting the powerful intention of acceptance and living in the present moment.** It is letting go of the past and having no thoughts of the future. Acceptance includes not seeking a cure or the resolutions of a difficult relationship or a burdensome state of mind. Levels of attachments tend to strengthen when death approaches and with awareness and a strong belief a return to a peaceful state can occur. People who have had a near death experience no longer fear death. Music, poetry, and inspirational sayings from a chosen teacher raises energy vibrations.

5. **The level of attachment will be reflected in the level of death anxiety.** Recall and breathe in the suffering of others and mindfully send out loving compassion and intention. This is a time for forgiveness of self and others. Some people express it as 'letting go.' The place of death is not important when the soul is at peace and the illusion of this physical world fades away. When death is accepted as a stage of the soul's journey, and not an end, anxiety diminishes and gives way to faith and feelings of Oneness. Seasoned practitioners prefer to die alone while others will appreciate having a person remind them of comforting spiritual explorations.

Funeral Considerations (see Appendix for Funeral Planning)

Ken chose to die at home and because his widow was in her nineties and blind, the funeral was held at home so that she could be part of it. She felt the coffin and placed her flowers on it. After the simple service, those present added garden flowers to those of the widow. As the funeral car drove away, a homing pigeon was released. It circled the house several times before symbolically flying away.

Bob was a very competitive man, successful in sport and business. He planted a tree when his leukaemia was diagnosed and enjoyed the time spent in his garden. His wife very thoughtfully arranged a simple spray from his garden on the coffin. It contained flowers, sprigs from his much-loved tree and tomato bushes. His funeral service was held at his Church with a private cremation.

Betty was a farmer and had a very strong character. She faced death bravely after a planned final week on a houseboat with two special friends. Betty wanted a no-nonsense burial and service at a country grave site. Another grave side service was preceded with a get together at home where friends circled the coffin and sang favourite hymns.

Many families choose to have a service at the crematorium or funeral chapel with refreshments to follow in a side room. Some have an open coffin prior to the service for final goodbyes. One widower chose to have a memorial service following a private cremation. The memorial service depicted displays of his wife's needlework.

The nurse attended a funeral in a Nursing Home chapel. As she entered, she was impressed by the line-up of walking frames at the back of the chapel and thought how wonderful for the funeral to be held in the Nursing Home so that other residents were able to say their good-byes and be reassured.

Other comments heard by the nurse include: "I have his ashes waiting until I die - then they can be mixed and given to the grandchildren." "I don't know where to scatter the ashes - he loved the Flinders Ranges in South Australia, but he also loved the beach and would run along it - loving the feel of the wind."

By assisting me wash the person who has died, relatives and friends have expressed feelings of privilege as well as having visible signs that life has ceased. One middle aged woman said that she had fears of her husband being put in a refrigerator while still being alive. By helping the nurse at the time of death she could see the blood pooling in the lower half of the body and see at first hand that circulation had ceased. There is also a natural curiosity to be satisfied: "Doesn't he look dignified." "The lines in the face have disappeared." "How beautiful she looks." "The struggling to breathe and the discomforts of the failing body have given way to the shell." "I'm so pleased that you encouraged me to stay after he had died." - are a few of the comments I have heard.

Most times there is no need to hurry the body away. One widow who slept beside the body of her husband for one more night said: "I knew he wasn't breathing but I just wanted him for one more night - then I was happy for them to take him away". A young woman slept beside her sister who had died early in the evening and imagined that her sister was up on the ceiling looking down on them. A son flew from interstate and hurried to the hostel room where his mother had died the previous evening. He said: "I felt part of her death and it was easier to say goodbye in the room which had become her home".

When it comes to dressing the body of the person who has died, it is important to consider the character of that person. For example, one woman who was dying said she liked the hymn "All things bright and beautiful." Her dressing gown was bright and beautiful. It was covered with flowers and it seemed appropriate to dress her in that same gown after death. She was also an ardent football fan, so her red bed-socks were put on in memory of her team's colours. One family insisted that their father and husband be fully dressed - even to the belt that they said they had all received at one time!

Leaving the face uncovered and the hands in a natural position for holding is usually appreciated. It is important to close the mouth and eyelids. A lipstick holder wrapped in a lace handkerchief may be used to close the mount of a little lady, or even a thin cake of soap wrapped in a handkerchief or face washer may be effective. The circle of cardboard from the inside of a toilet roll has also been useful. It can be hidden with a scarf or fresh linen. Flowers, cards, prayer books, various mementos from the person's life may surround the person or be placed on the pillows or fresh bed linen. Little rituals like placing a dimmed light by the bedside, closing the curtains, removing the signs of illness, and placing chairs around the bed or facilitating the holding of hands around the bed for a moment of silence, spontaneous or formal prayer can be loving touches.

Dreams and a Sense of Presence

When asked how she felt about sleeping in the bed where her husband had died one young widow replied: "I will never sell that bed - I sleep on his side for that is where I feel closest to him." "I often have a conversation with him - I feel that he is right by my side." "I had this strange experience when I was mowing the lawn... I smelt the smoke of his cigarettes."

Several nights after Bea died, her friend had a dream in which she appeared and told him about a piece of music and where it could be found. The friend said: "There is no known explanation for the discovery". An eighty-year-old woman described a dream she had four years after her husband's death. She had been called by a neighbour to open her gates and as she stepped outside the house a man appeared by her side. She looked up at the roof and there was a gush of water from the roof. With the man she walked toward the gate and opened the left side, and the man went out. When she woke, she went to see that the gate was indeed closed but said that from that time on she had a sense of being empowered to cope on her own - she felt her husband's spirit had finally left her.

A daughter had her garden specially landscaped so that her mother's oriental shrine could be placed in the bottom of the garden for her private talks. Recordings of serendipitous events are many and there are often questions regarding life after death and different beliefs. One pragmatic eighty-year-old doctor said: "It is time for me to walk away from the tribe. I'm a scientist and believe that when a person is dead that is the finish." Others will have a profound faith in seeing a place where there are many mansions. I considered it to be important to acknowledge the place of mystery and the spiritual dimension as simply as possible. Most importantly what were the person's wishes?

Tears

It is said that tears are the 'sprinkler system' of the soul. Feelings of sadness, loneliness or bewilderment often touch deeper meaning in life issues which are by-passed in the everyday bustle.

Fred put on a tough front when his wife died. It was my habit to contact family on the anniversary of the death. When Fred received his anniversary card, he phoned and accepted an invitation to have a cup of tea with me. When he arrived, he remarked: "I came because I wanted to see what was in it for you!" How perceptive! We made friends and he reported that he had joined an elderly citizen's club and was getting on with life.

"I've got David in the wardrobe - do you want to see?" As David had died two years ago and not wanting to doubt the supernatural, I just blinked. There on a shelf, neatly packaged, were David's ashes - "It was strange bringing him home in a carry bag - I had to wait until I was ready."

Each little death/disappointment in a person's life gives that person strength to face the future losses. What is important is not only to identify but also to understand what is going on in the inner life. "You know when Harry died, what came up so vividly for me were the feelings on leaving Italy twenty years ago."

One day I returned home to find some pumpkins and a bag of oranges on my doorstep. A phone call confirmed that the son of a patient who had recently died was in town. "She was always in tune with nature - wasn't it appropriate the way she died at sunset. Remember the tear that settled in her eye when she stopped breathing?" I remembered that when I had prepared this wise mother after death - including a camellia from the garden - the son had taken a photograph. "I don't know what the rest of the family will think but I want to remember her this way too."

Technology

Hopefully, the development of technology will allow more time for building relationships which are the foundation of life as well as enable people to stay connected and enjoy podcasts and videos from many parts of the world. We are all one!

Karen was a medical orderly on board ship. She left the ship to care for her mother who was dying at home. Everything she did was precise and orderly. An example was her documentation of her mother's daily care. Another part of her character was to practise meditation and give as much help as possible to her mother on her final voyage. The mother did not like the thought of being connected to a syringe driver. Karen asked: "What is the need when we are here all the time?" The need for continuous medication was acknowledged and Karen marked a piece of tape with divisions and times to be placed on the syringe containing the medication. This was manually advanced and recorded and the mother found this personal method of delivery of medication much more acceptable.

"This remote-control doorbell allows me to potter in the shed or garden with the reassurance that I can hear Lois when she pushes the button that I've taped for easy reach by her pillow. It is simple, effective, inexpensive and gives so much peace of mind! We're both in our eighties and private people – One day, I'll call you for some help with the nights."

"Every time we turn her, she hurts - but we are worried about her skin and feel awful about moving her." I produced a plastic mattress with small tubes for alternating air pressure. This was covered with a medical woollen overlay which would not restrict the pressure changes and would allow the air to circulate against the skin. The patient was able to lie in the favourite position for up to eight hours without being moved. Patients need to be made comfortable so that they can mentally prepare to die without distracting discomfort. The essence or psyche of the person needs to be afforded as much uninterrupted peace as possible. Technology is used for sound reproduction, controlling the air temperature and communication devices - just to name a few. We are in the age of technology which is making us all more responsible for our own health care.

There is also an increase in psychic sensitivities which can manifest in all sorts of ways; and changed attitudes to religion. After near-death experiences people generally tended to move away from the path of formalised religion to a more personal relationship with their God, favouring practices such as meditation, non-formula prayer and a general quest for spiritual values. They tended to feel that during their near-death experience (NDE) they had experienced a direct experience of God or a Higher Power and that that relationship was still ongoing in their everyday lives. By far most experiencers described themselves more as 'spiritual' than religious. For instance, Daphne said,

> *I don't like the word 'religious' because it has church connotations. I think 'spiritual'*
> *is the stronger because it's only between me and the Higher Intelligence. 'Religious'*
> *concerns religion whereas 'spiritual' concerns your own spirit and your own will and soul*
> *environment.*

And Cora expressed her ambivalence:

Choice is empowering and when death ceases to be a taboo subject, options which have personal meaning may be considered. Making an Advance Care Directive and leaving a Funeral Planning Guide demonstrate consideration for those left behind.

Summary

From reading this book you will appreciate that I have a deep appreciation for health care that is holistic in nature and encourages self-care and responsibility. This is the era of energy medicine – a time when soul energy, which underpins all life – be it an individual or a corporate entity - is being appreciated.

Energy, with its differing vibrations, flows through the body and influences thoughts and emotions and vice versa. When its role is understood, a new perspective on health care can emerge. This is the same energy that leaves the body when a person, pet or any living thing dies. It cannot be destroyed but it can be transformed.

For example, peace and harmony can be felt in certain places at a given time. If the space becomes occupied by angry and manipulative energy, the peace and harmony vanish. The same happens to the energy in a person's body. Energy which flows through the body may become blocked, or affected positively or negatively, by emotions and thoughts. The result may be seen and felt when a person becomes moody, dark and vengeful rather than light, loving and compassionate.

Triggers that have an effect on thoughts and emotions come from many sources. The triggers may be conscious or unconscious and relate to events in this lifetime or a past lifetime. Because soul energy can never die, another mode of existence occurs after death. This is a reality experienced by those who feel the presence of a person they felt a deep connection with and has died.

Many philosophers and poets have written about soul, life and meaning from the earliest recordings to the present day. The New Age Movement began in the 1960s and gave a new language to the truths to be found in holy books. Eastern and Western thought is combining to form different ways of viewing wellness and introducing words like karma, chakras, and aura.

A bridge is being built between western medicine, traditional medicine, and inner self/energy medicine.

Practical Information

Health team

Registered Nurse or Doula:

____

Phone:

____

After hours phone:

____

General Practitioner (family doctor):

____

Address:

____

Postcode:

____

Phone:

____

After hours phone:

____

Medical Specialist:

____

Address:

____

Postcode:

____

Phone:

____

After hours phone:

____

Medical Specialist:

____

Address:

____

Postcode:

____

Phone:

____

After hours phone:

____

Local Chemist:

____

Address:

____

Postcode:

____

Phone:

____

Deliver: ☐ No ☐ Yes, Day:

Equipment hire details:

____

Phone:

____

A/C responsibility:

____

Security details:

____

Phone:

____

Family members or supportive friends

Name:

____

Relationship:

____

Address:

____

Postcode:

____

Home phone:

____

Work phone:

____

Email/fax:

____

Mobile:

____

Name:

____

Relationship:

____

Address:

____

Postcode:

____

Home phone:

____

Work phone:

____

Email/fax:

____

Mobile:

____

Primary contact/Substitute Decision Maker/Medical Power of Attorney:

____

Other health professional/Complementary Therapist:

____

Address:

____

Postcode:

____

Phone:

____

After hours phone:

____

Religion/Spiritual support:

____

Address:

____

Postcode:

____

Phone:

____

After hours phone:

____

Legal details:

____

Legal details:

____

☐ Will   ☐ Enduring Power of Attorney   ☐ Medical Power of Attorney

☐ Legal Guardian   ☐ Advance Care Directive

Details:

____

____

____

____

Funeral Planning Guide:

____

Notes:

____

Allergies:

____

Diagnosis:

____

Previous medical/ surgical history:

____

Current health concerns:

____

Ambulance membership: ☐ Yes   ☐ No

Access cab: ☐ Yes   ☐ No

Details:

Details:

____

____

____

____

Medication record for self-administration

Date	Medication	Dose	Route	Frequency	Effect

Purpose of medication:

____

Notes:

____

____

Date	Medication	Dose	Route	Frequency	Effect

Purpose of medication:

____

Notes:

____

____

Date	Medication	Dose	Route	Frequency	Effect

Purpose of medication:

____

Notes:

____

____

Date	Medication	Dose	Route	Frequency	Effect

Purpose of medication:

____

Notes:

____

____

Date	Medication	Dose	Route	Frequency	Effect

Purpose of medication:

____

Notes:

____

____

Date	Medication	Dose	Route	Frequency	Effect

Purpose of medication:

____

Notes:

____

____

Date	Medication	Dose	Route	Frequency	Effect

Purpose of medication:

____

Notes:

____

____

Date	Medication	Dose	Route	Frequency	Effect

Purpose of medication:

____

Notes:

____

____

Date	Medication	Dose	Route	Frequency	Effect

Purpose of medication:

____

Notes:

____

____

Please Note: Ensure your medications are clearly labelled and that you have adequate lighting when you take your medicine or tablets. Take only as per instructions and ask before taking old or other people's medications. If tablets are difficult to swallow ask your nurse if they may be crushed and taken with e.g. ice cream, honey, fruit puree. Not all tablets may be crushed as they may be formulated for sustained, slow release. Keep your medicine in a childproof medicine cupboard or safe place. Check expiry date of medication and that you have an adequate supply for when the chemist may be closed. Inquire about pre-filled daily packs from your chemist or nurse.

Contents

INTRODUCTION

"Nothing in life is to be feared – merely understood" – Marie Curie

When a person feels their life span is coming to an end, they begin to think about 'putting their affairs in order' to make it easier for those who are left behind.

It has been said that the funeral is for those who are left behind as it is a public expression of their grief. While that is the case, a person making end of life choices (perhaps when drawing up an Advance Care Directive) may wish to share their wishes and values, as well as provide a record of practical information.

End of Life preparations might include a Living Wake

This is a new concept for some people as they make plans for the last phase of life. However, there are many benefits to be gained by including the concept in this Funeral Guide.

This is an example of a Living Wake:

> The author recalls that this idea came from the family of a ninety-year-old woman who was dying in a nursing home. One son had organised a birthday party for her and proudly told his mother's palliative care nurse how his mother had enjoyed hearing the story of her life which was read at the event.

> The nurse remembered the day the woman died and recalled that she was certainly, and uncannily, at peace. She had chosen the nightdress she would wear after her shower that morning and reported to the nurse that she felt this was her special day. She bravely whispered goodbyes to her interstate and country family on the telephone before falling into a deep asleep. She seemed to have an intuitive, or non-rational soul knowing, that it was her time.

> The palliative care nurse's role was to honour the process in a non-judgemental way and to keep the atmosphere calm and loving - knowing that palliative care neither hastens nor postpones death. The elderly woman's breathing became irregular and quite shallow. It was a deep sleep and one that would end some hours later.

> The room filled with family as she took her last breath. The way this woman left this physical life could only be described as a good and timely death. The family wished that more people could have the same experience.

How to word the invitation if you choose to have a Living Wake.

For example, "Nothing would give me greater pleasure than to be together one more time. Please come to my Living Wake…"

This booklet is designed to serve as a guide for recording a person's thoughts on how their funeral, which is the celebration of their life, may be conducted. In an ideal world a palliative care professional or close family member may be available as a sounding board to assist with choices and decisions.

When a person dies it is a time for sadness, confusion, and change. Leaving a useful guide of practical information is one way a person can show thoughtfulness for those left behind.

PERSONAL DETAILS

Full Name ....

Address .... Postcode ....

Telephone .... Email ....

Employer...

Occupation ....

Place of Birth ....

Country of Birth ....

Date of Birth Religion ....

Next of Kin ....

Marital Status: Married ☐ Never

- Married

- Widowed ☐ Divorced

- Married more than once

To whom married ....

Given Maiden Name ....

Date and Place of Marriage / / ....

To whom married ....

Given Maiden Name..

Date and Place of Marriage / / ....

To whom married ....

Given Maiden Name..

Date and Place of Marriage / / ....

To whom married ....

Given Maiden Name..

DONATION OF BODY TO SCIENCE

I wish to donate my body for the purpose of Medical Research Information

on this is kept ....

My family are aware of my intentions Yes ☐   No ☐

ORGAN DONOR

I am a registered organ donor.

Details of this are kept ....

My family are aware of my intentions Yes ☐   No ☐

MY DOCTOR'S DETAILS

Name...

Telephone ....

Do not stand at my grave and weep, I am not there, I do not sleep. I am a

thousand winds that blow, I am the diamond glints on snow,

I am the sunlight on ripened grain,

I am the gentle autumn rain, when you awaken in the mornings hush,

I am the swift uplifting rush, of quiet birds in circled flight,

I am the soft stars that shine at night.

Do not stand at my grave and cry I am not there I did not die (Martha Benamati)

FUNERAL ARRANGEMENTS

Preferred Funeral Director

....

Telephone

....

I have a prepaid funeral plan with

....

These are the details

....

....

....

I have a preference for: Burial ☐   Cremation ☐

I wish my funeral to be:

Private ☐ Public ☐ Funeral With coffin present ☐   Without coffin ☐

With private burial and service of celebration to be held at:

Funeral Home...

Memorial Park ....

Crematorium – Chapel

Name..

Church ....

Home ....

Graveside ....

Type of Service

Memorial Service with the involvement of family if they wish

- Wake

- Requiem Mass

- Order of Service

Preferred Minister/Celebrant ....

INTERMENT DETAILS

I have an allotment   Yes ☐ No ☐

New License ☐   Opening ☐ Re-opening ☐   Depth ....

License No ....

Section .... Path ....Lot No ....

Lessee ....

Lessee's address ....

Name of last INTERMENT ....

Date of last INTERMENT..

Return Leaset Yes ☐ No ☐

Lease extension request   Yes ☐ No ☐ - Years ....

CREMATED REMAINS – PLACEMENT INSTRUCTIONS

I would like my ashes to be scattered/or placed

....

I would like the following inscription to be placed on the Headstone:

....

....

....

....

(Some people just wish a name, date of birth and date of death while others may
wish to have a description of character and achievements. It is all personal and
family members may have their suggestions. It is good to have the conversation and
so normalize the place of death in life.)

SUGGESTED PALL BEARERS

Name ....

Name ....

Name ....

Name ....

Name ....

Name ....

Suggestions for personal memoir

1. These things I have loved in life...
2. These experiences I have cherished...
3. These beliefs I have outgrown...
4. These ideas have liberated me...
5. These convictions I have lived by...
6. These insights I have arrived at...
7. These risks I have taken...
8. These things I have lived for...
9. These sufferings have had silver linings...
10. Life has taught me these lessons...
11. These people have shaped my life...
12. These holy readings have helped me...
13. These things I regret about my life...
14. These are my life's achievements...

Music that has been inspiring in my lifetime:

....

....

....

Readings/poetry that have lifted me when I wondered about the meaning of life

....

....

....

Photographs representing the significant events of my life may be shown during the funeral

....

....

....

My preferred selection can be found:

....

....

....

FLORAL ART/MEMORABILIA

My favorite flowers are: ....

What kind of floral art/ memorabilia would you like to be placed on top of the coffin?

....

Is there any charity or organization you would prefer donations in lieu of flowers to go to?

....

If you have flowers on your coffin where would you like these to go after the funeral?

....

INFORMATION FOR ADMINISTRATOR OF MY ESTATE

FINANCIAL DETAILS

Home (*owned - singly / jointly*) ....

Mortgaged to ....

Insurance Policy on home with ....

Bank Accounts/Credit Cards/Online Financial Transactions/Passwords

Name Branch of Bank	Account Number	Account Name

Online account details

Password storage ....

Superannuation Fund

Name of Company/Manager ....

Address ....

....

Telephone No .... Account No ....

Life Insurance

Name of Company/Manager ....

Address ....

....

Telephone No .... Policy No ....

Pension(s)

Pension No ....

Pension No ....

Pension No ....

Medical Plan Details: ....

Agency Support ....

Private Health Insurance

Name of Fund ....

Policy No ....

Telephone No ....

The following documents can be found:

Advance Care Directive

....

Enduring Power of Attorney

....

Original & Copies of Will

....

Original ....

Copies ....

Executor/s of Will

....

Birth Certificate

....

Marriage Certificate/s

....

Savings Bank Book / Cheque Book etc

....

Securities / Share Certificates / Bonds etc

....

Personal Insurance Policies

....

Medical Benefits / Friendly Society / Medicare Cards

....

....

Title Deed for each piece of Real Estate

____

Home ____

Other ____

Insurance Policies

Home ____

Other ____

Title Deed for each piece of Real Estate

____

Home ____

Other ____

Motor Vehicle Registration Certificate

Motor Vehicle Comprehensive Insurance Policy

____

Service Record & Discharge Certificate

____

Pension / Concession Card (s)

____

Gas, electricity and phone companies

....

Foreign pension authority (Centrelink's International Services 131 673)

....

Memberships

....

Any other important Documents (*specify*)

....

....

....

Personal Details included in this booklet will need to be supplied to the Funeral Director so keep it handy for your next of kin

Full Name of Father

Surname..

Given names ....

Occupation ....

Full Name of Mother

Surname..

Given names ....

Occupation ....

Don't Cry for me

Don't cry for me now I have died, for I'm still here I'm by your side,
My body's gone but my soul's is here, please don't shed another tear,
I am still here I'm all around, only my body lies in the ground.
I am the snowflake that kisses your nose,
I am the frost, that nips your toes.
I am the sun, bringing you light,
I am the star, shining so bright.
I am the rain, refreshing the earth,
I am the laughter,
I am the mirth.
I am the bird, up in the sky,
I am the cloud, that's drifting by.
I am the thoughts, inside your head,
While I'm still there, I can't be dead.
Author unknown.

QUESTIONS THE FAMILY MAY BE ASKED BY THE FUNERAL DIRECTOR

Would you like a viewing?

Who will be identifying the deceased?

What clothing is to be worn by the deceased?

NOTE

How the body of the person who has died is prepared will vary and may depend on the place of death. The place of death may be the person's own home (with or without palliative care), a hospice, a health care facility or if by accident, or request, under the direction of the funeral home.

Families may wish to take part in rituals such as helping wash and dress the body. When death occurs at home, they might wish to form a guard of honour as the coffin is taken away by the chosen funeral director.

Some families placed a sprig of flowers or a favourite hat or cap on the trolley as it is taken to the funeral vehicle. It is the beginning of a special time of grieving when a person is remembered for what they meant to each other.

OTHER CONSDIERATIONS

Rings or other valuables - Return/Leave

Does the person who has died have any implants? YES/NO

Type.. Situated ....

Coffin Name Plate Inscription ....

BADGE/CROSS/ NIL (circle one) to be placed on Coffin lid

Is the deceased a Returned Service Person - Yes ☐ No ☐

If yes please consider the following:

Military Service with

....

Display Medals: Yes ☐ Nos ☐			
Flag:	Yes ☐ No ☐ Type:	Last Post:	Yes ☐ No ☐
Ode:	Yes ☐ No ☐	Masonic:	Yes ☐ No ☐
Poppies:	Yes ☐ No ☐	Acacia:	Yes ☐ No ☐

Funeral Notice

The next of kin and family will need to consider the Funeral notice. Some people choose to have notices made public following the funeral and others may wish to give notice with consideration for those who may have a distance to travel. The funeral people will be helpful in placing such notices

Message

....

....

....

CHECKLIST OF PLACES TO NOTIFY FOLLOWING THE DEATH

A doctor will need to certify the death. If the death is expected and occurs at home do not call the ambulance. Once the death is certified a funeral director will remove the body and assist with the legal notifications and arrangements.

When a relative, friend or neighbour dies, this checklist may help you to remember the many people and offices that must be advised. All of these may not be applicable to everyone's circumstances.

- Decide on the time and place to meet with the funeral director

- When choosing a day and time for the funeral consider if time for travel needs consideration

- Discus with the funeral director if the service is to be recorded and what is to be printed on the Order of Service and catering requirements if needed.

- Notify pallbearers. Make a list of immediate family, close friends and employer or business colleagues. Notify each by phone.

- Check the Funeral Plan for wishes regarding flowers or donations in lieu to a chosen charity

- Write the eulogy or life story e.g. age, place of birth, cause of death, occupation, college degrees, memberships held, military service outstanding work, list of survivors in immediate family

- Check Funeral Plan for wishes regarding photographs/memorabilia

- Consider how the eulogy is delivered. It may be shared between the celebrant and family/ friends

- Notify lawyer and executor of the Will

- Arrange for members of family or close friends to take turns answering door or phone, keeping careful record of calls.

- Arrange appropriate childcare if needed

- Take precaution against thieves

- Arrange care of pets

- Coordinate a supply of food for those in deep grief

- Consider special needs of the household such as cleaning and laundry

- Arrange for hospitality for visiting relatives or friends

- Plan for disposition of flowers if that was stated in the Funeral Plan

- Prepare notice for newspapers observing any personal instruction

- Prepare list of persons to receive acknowledgements for gifts of food, flowers, etc. Send appropriate acknowledgements (Can be written notes, printed acknowledgements, or some of each)

- Check promptly on all debts and instalments payments. If necessary, explain a possible delay

- Check on income for survivors

- Check carefully the following and notify accordingly.

Bank (including all credit cards)	Meals on Wheels
Cancel any appointments with doctors, hairdressers etc	Medicare
Cancel newspapers, bread, milk deliveries	Mortality Fund
Chemist	Optometrist
Church	Physiotherapist
Clubs	Post Office (regarding mail)
Department of Motor Vehicles (re registration and driver's licence)	Podiatrist
Department store accounts	Private Health Fund
Electoral Office Manager	School
Electricity	Senior Citizens Club
Employer	Social Security (pension benefit, family benefit)
Gas	Solicitor / Public Trustee
Home Nursing Service	Superannuation Fund
Home Care	Taxation Office
Hospice / Hospital Ward	Telephone provider
Insurance Company (including care insurance) for cancellation and available refund	Union
Landlord (if renting)	Veteran Affairs
Library	Water Rates
Local Council (re rates etc, if owner)	

"There are no goodbyes for us.
Wherever you are, you will always be in my heart."

~ Gandhi

PRACTICAL HINTS FOR THE BEREAVED

*I need someone who believes that the sun will rise again but who does not fear my darkness.
Someone who can point out the rocks in my way without making me a child by carrying me.
Someone who can stand in thunder and watch the lightning and believe in a rainbow.*

Fr Joe Mahoney

The following highlights a few important matters to consider during bereavement. Each person is different so beware of ready-made solutions. The following are suggestions to consider – they may or may not fit your situation

Psychological

Accepting support at the time of bereavement can difficult. So much of the journey of grief does need to be made alone but accepting a kindness from another at this time is what makes community. Do accept offers of practical assistance.

While you may feel pressured to put on a brave front, it is important to make your feelings known by expressing your feelings to those you trust.

Often numbness sees us through the first few days or weeks. Do not be too surprised if a let-down comes later.

Many people are emotionally upset during bereavement than at any other times in their lives and are frightened by this. Be aware that severe upset is not unusual and if you are alarmed, seek a professional opinion.

Whether you feel you need to be alone or accompanied – make it known. Needing company is common and does *not* mean you will *always* be dependent on it.

There is no set time limit for grieving; it varies from person to person, depending on individual circumstances. Be kind to yourself. Be forgiving of self and others. Accept and express feelings.

Physical

- It is easy to neglect yourself when you are grieving.

- Smile and reinforce your worth in whatever role you choose

- Exercise in nature if possible. You may need to feel alone, or you may seek company.

- You may be more susceptible to disease as stress influences the immune system

- Remember the whole person – healthy mind, healthy body, healthy spirit

- Try to eat reasonably even if there is no enjoyment in it

- Although sleep may be disturbed, try to get adequate rest

- It is healthy to cry; "tears are the sprinkler system of the soul"

- If you have symptoms, get a doctor to check them out

- If people urge you to see your doctor, do so even if it does not make sense to you at the time

Social

Friends and family are often most available early in bereavement and less so later. It is important to be able to reach out to them when you need them. Don't wait for them to guess your needs. They will often guess incorrectly and be too late.

During a period of grief, it can be difficult to judge new relationships. Do not be afraid of them, yet it is usually wise not to rush into them. It may feel like there is a void that begs to be filled but remember that emotions are not always rational (or when we are emotional, we are not in our 'right' mind and this may cause more pain if we are unconsciously projecting feeling we had for one person onto another person.)

Someone who is not too close to you but who is willing to listen may be particularly helpful when discerning the nature of a new relationship.

No-one will substitute for your loss. Try to enjoy people as they are. Do not avoid social contacts because of the imperfections in those you meet.

Sometimes, in an effort to stop the pain of grief, people turn towards replacing the lost person (e.g. through adoption of a child, remarriage) too soon. It is hard, though, to see new relationships objectively if you are still actively grieving and this kind of solution may only lead to other problems.

Try to make it clear to children that sadness is perfectly normal and that neither theirs nor yours need to be hidden. It is important that periods of happiness are enjoyed and not a cause of guilty feelings

Economic

Avoid hasty decisions. Try not to make major life decisions within the first year unless absolutely necessary.

Be aware of internet offers and respond only to known and trusted sources.

In general, most people find it best to remain settled in familiar surroundings until they can consider their future calmly.

Don't be afraid to seek good advice. Usually, it is wise to get more than one opinion before making decisions. Do not make any major financial decisions without talking them over with trustworthy professional people.

Having a job or doing voluntary work in the community can be helpful when you are ready, but it is important not to overextend yourself and become so busy that grief becomes buried. Gardening is therapeutic. Age and circumstances of the loss all play a part.

Foster the relationships with family, friends, and work. Keeping busy can be a way of avoiding the pain of grief. A normal part of the grieving process is to get on with life and another part is to visit the grief in our hearts. There needs to be a balance.

Spiritual

Personal faith is frequently a major source of comfort during bereavement. However, for some, maintaining faith may be difficult during this period of loss. Either reaction may occur and both are consistent with spiritual growth. Spiritual growth occurs when a person considers what is essential and nurturing and what is superficial in their life. Bereavement is a time for looking for meaning and connectedness.

You may feel the need to go within and make time for reflection and being still. Many seek a connection with nature when soul is involved and enjoy a walk in a garden or by the sea. You might find it helpful to write your memories of the person you have lost and live your life as though they were still present.

Connecting with the 'God within' is a time when rituals and symbols speak louder than words. A piece of music or a poem can speak to the depths of a soul. Culture will play an important role even if you feel you have outgrown those who gave you early nurturing.

It is a time for photographs and remembering when... looking for the gift and seeing the person who has died in a new light... It is a time for prayer and meditation and connection with a Higher Power or loving energy. This may in solitude or with a community.

GRIEF BY GWEN FLOWERS

I had my own notion of grief.
I thought it was the sad time
That followed the death of someone you
love.
And you had to push through it
To get to the other side.
But I'm learning there is no other side.
There is no pushing through.
But rather,
There is absorption.
Adjustment.
Acceptance.
And grief is not something you complete,
But rather, you endure.
Grief is not a task to finish
And move on,
But an element of yourself-
An alteration of your being.
A new way of seeing.
A new definition of self.

LIST OF PEOPLE TO BE NOTIFIED FOLLOWING MY DEATH

Name ....

Address ....

Telephone No .... Mobile .... Email ....

Relationship ....

Name ....

Address ....

Telephone No .... Mobile .... Email ....

Relationship ....

Name ....

Address ....

Telephone No .... Mobile .... Email ....

Relationship ....

Name ....

Address ....

Telephone No .... Mobile .... Email ....

Relationship ....

Name ....

Address ....

Telephone No .... Mobile .... Email ....

Relationship ....

*"Fear of death exists only in those
who are ignorant of their own souls"*
-Pythagoras

(Johnsen, Linda. (2016) Lost Masters, New World Library,
An Eckhart Tolle edition, USA p 19)